The Jungle

KEVIN ANGERO

Published by KEVIN ANGERO, 2025.

THE JUNGLE

First edition. April 2, 2025.

ISBN: 979-8230201625

Written by KEVIN ANGERO.

Also by KEVIN ANGERO

The Jungle

Table of Contents

To the dreamers, the strategists, and the survivors—

This book is for those who dare to navigate the financial wilderness, who adapt, endure, and thrive despite the challenges. To everyone who has faced droughts, outmaneuvered predators, and fought relentlessly for their financial future—may this guide be your compass in the ever-changing jungle of wealth.

To my family, friends, and mentors—your wisdom, support, and encouragement have been my foundation. And to the readers, may you find strength in knowledge, courage in action, and prosperity in the journey ahead.

Welcome to the jungle.

"In the jungle, only the sharpest survive. The patient hunter feasts, the reckless prey falls, and the wise traveler learns to read the signs of the land. Finance is no different—it's a game of instincts, strategy, and resilience."

— Unknown

Chapter 1: Sunrise

In the jungle, the sunrise is more than just a beautiful sight—it's a signal of survival. As the first light cracks the horizon, it wakes the entire ecosystem into action. The chirping of birds, the rustling of leaves, and the stretching shadows signal that a new day has begun, and with it comes fresh opportunities, but also new dangers. For the antelope, the early hours mean feeding in the safety of morning light. For the lion, it marks the start of the hunt—using the cover of the rising sun to stalk its prey.

Everything depends on timing. The predators know the hunt is best in the cool hours of dawn, while the prey understands that their chance to graze safely is brief before the heat and hunger of the day grow stronger. Each animal, whether hunter or hunted, has learned to make the most of these first few hours. In this short window, every decision can lead to survival or failure. The jungle in the morning is a battlefield where only the prepared and vigilant thrive.

Sometimes in the jungle, the sunrise doesn't just signal the start of the day—it marks a critical shift. For some, like the antelope, it's the opportunity to venture out and feed, capitalizing on the safety that daylight provides. But for others, like the nocturnal hunters—the leopards, hyenas, and owls—the sunrise is the signal to retreat, having worked through the cover of darkness. For these creatures, the day is a time to rest, recharge, and plan for the next hunt.

It's a balance. While the sun offers new possibilities for some, it signals the end of opportunity for others. In the hours before dawn, the nocturnal hunters have already made their moves, silently stalking the unsuspecting. By the time the sun rises, they have fed, strategized, and now retreat into the shadows, conserving their energy for when darkness falls again. Their success depends on knowing when to act and, equally important when to pull back and rest.

The same principle exists in finance. While one investor sees the dawn of a new opportunity—a chance to buy into a rising market—another might recognize that it's time to step back, take profits, and rest until the next big wave. Warren Buffet often talks about the importance of patience, of waiting for the right moment to strike, much like the leopard that hunts at night and rests when the sun shines. Understanding when to act and when to pause is key to long-term success, whether you're navigating the jungle or the financial world.

Not every sunrise demands action. Sometimes, it's a reminder to rest, review, and prepare for the next cycle. Knowing when to advance and when to retreat is what separates those who survive from those who thrive.

AWAKENING AWARENESS: UNDERSTANDING YOUR FINANCIAL LANDSCAPE.

The jungle comes alive with the first touch of sunlight, casting a golden glow across the vast landscape. In this fleeting moment, every creature becomes acutely aware of its surroundings. For some, the dawn brings clarity—a chance to see the terrain, assess the dangers, and plan the day's moves. The once-shadowed paths now come into focus. The antelope now knows where it can graze safely, and the lion sees its target more clearly. With the dawn comes awareness—an understanding of the opportunities and threats that lie ahead.

For you, the sunrise in the financial world can be just as revealing. When you wake up to your financial reality, you gain a newfound clarity. Maybe for the first time, you see the full landscape: your spending habits, your savings potential, your investments, and your debt. Just like the animals of the jungle, your awareness is your greatest tool for survival.

Perhaps you've been wandering in the dark, unsure of where your money is going or how to make it grow. The dawn of financial awareness sheds light on everything. It's that moment when you open your bank statement, check your investments, or finally sit down to create a budget. Suddenly, things become clear—the jungle is no longer a place of confusion but of opportunity.

Why Awareness Matters

In the jungle, ignorance is a death sentence. A zebra unaware of a stalking predator won't survive the day. The same applies to your financial life. If you don't know your financial status—how much you spend, how much you save, and where your money goes—you can't make the right moves. Awareness is the foundation for building wealth.

Think of it like this: You wouldn't drive a car with your eyes closed, so why would you navigate your financial life blindly? When you become aware of your financial landscape, you can make informed decisions—whether that means cutting back on unnecessary expenses, starting to invest, or finding new ways to grow your income.

Now let's dive into three steps that can help you awaken your financial awareness like lions, elephants, wildebeests, and leopards become aware before starting their day at dawn.

Financial Self-Assessment: Taking Stock at Dawn

As the sun rises higher over the jungle, the creatures take a moment to assess their surroundings. The antelope, aware of its speed and agility, moves confidently across the plains. The lion, recognizing its strength, chooses to conserve energy for a well-planned hunt. Every animal knows its limits and capabilities—this is the essence of survival.

In the financial world, the first step of your journey begins with self-assessment. Just like the animals of the jungle take stock of their abilities, you must take a hard look at your financial standing. Where are you right now? Do you have savings? Are you drowning in debt? Do you understand your income, expenses, and financial habits? This moment of reflection is your dawn, your starting point.

Consider the story of Elon Musk before founding Tesla and SpaceX. After selling his stake in PayPal, Musk faced the ultimate self-assessment—he could play it safe with his fortune or risk it all on two ventures that could change the world. He chose the latter, but not without fully understanding the magnitude of his risk. Self-assessment allowed him to take the right steps and embrace calculated risks, ultimately leading to his massive success.

Awareness begins with looking inward and being brutally honest with yourself. This is how you chart a course for growth, because, in both finance and the jungle, knowing your strengths and weaknesses can be the difference between survival and extinction.

Understanding Assets, Liabilities, and Net Worth: Mapping Your Territory

In the jungle, survival isn't just about speed or strength; it's about understanding your territory. The elephant knows where to find water during a drought, while the leopard is aware of the best hunting grounds. These creatures thrive because they have a mental map of the resources available to them. They know where their strengths lie and what could hinder their survival.

In your financial life, this awareness translates into understanding your assets, liabilities, and net worth. Think of your assets—your savings, investments, property, or anything of value—as the fertile plains of the jungle, rich with opportunity. Your liabilities—debts, loans, and obligations—are like the predators lurking in the shadows, waiting to strike if you're not careful. And your net worth? That's your position in the jungle, your true strength, and where you stand amidst both resources and threats.

A perfect example of this awareness can be seen with Amazon's Jeff Bezos. In the early days, Bezos was fully aware of his company's assets and liabilities. By understanding where Amazon's value lay and where its risks were, he built one of the most successful businesses in the world. He reinvested profits and mitigated liabilities, allowing the company to thrive while other dot-com businesses were devoured by debt.

Just like in the jungle, knowing your financial landscape—your assets and liabilities—gives you the power to make informed decisions. You can't navigate without a map, and understanding these key components allows you to move confidently through your financial wilderness.

Recognizing Spending Habits: The Invisible Predator

In the jungle, not all dangers are visible. Sometimes, the biggest threat is something that creeps silently, catching the prey off guard. For many animals, the hidden predator is the deadliest of all. In your financial life, that hidden predator is often your spending habits—those little purchases and unconscious decisions that quietly drain your resources.

The wildebeest may appear safe as it grazes, but one wrong move, one lapse in vigilance, and it becomes easy prey. Similarly, unrecognized spending habits can quietly lead you toward financial ruin. Every small, unplanned purchase—whether it's your daily coffee habit, impulse buys, or unnecessary subscriptions—can slowly chip away at your financial health, just like a predator that stalks silently in the brush.

Take the story of Shaquille O'Neal, the legendary basketball player. Early in his career, Shaq admits to spending recklessly buying expensive cars, jewellery, and luxuries without a second thought. It wasn't until a financial advisor sat him down that he realized these spending habits were silently devouring his wealth. By recognizing the problem and adjusting his habits, Shaq was able to turn his finances around and build a lasting empire.

The key to success is awareness. In the same way a wildebeest must remain constantly alert to avoid predators, you must become aware of how you spend your money. Track it, understand it, and ask yourself: Are these expenses aligned with my goals, or are they slowly pulling me away from financial freedom? The invisible predator of unchecked spending can only be defeated through vigilance and conscious decision-making.

The Light of Awareness

In the jungle, awareness is everything. It separates those who thrive from those who fall prey. As the sun rises, the creatures of the wild wake up, assess their surroundings, understand their strengths, and become mindful of the dangers around them. Your financial life is no different.

When you conduct a financial self-assessment, you gain clarity about where you stand. When you map out your assets, liabilities, and net worth, you understand your position in the landscape. And when you recognize your spending habits, you remain vigilant against the silent predators that threaten your progress.

Just as the animals rely on their instincts, you must rely on your awareness. The sun has risen—now it's time for you to see clearly and take control.

SETTING INTENTIONS: DEFINING YOUR FINANCIAL GOALS

As the sun climbs higher in the sky, the jungle becomes a hub of activity. Each animal prepares for the day ahead with purpose and intention. The antelope browses for the best grass, while the lion gathers its strength for the hunt. This intentional preparation is crucial for their survival and success. Just as these creatures align their actions with their needs, you too must define your financial goals to chart a clear course on your journey.

1. Setting SMART Financial Goals: The Blueprint for Success

In the jungle, successful hunters don't just roam; they have a plan. The lion, for example, doesn't simply chase any animal in sight. Instead, it studies its target, calculating the risks and rewards before it leaps into action. In the same way, setting SMART (Specific, Measurable, Achievable, Relevant, Time-bound) financial goals provides a clear blueprint for your financial journey.

Imagine you want to save for a new car. Instead of saying, "I want to save money," a SMART goal might look like this: "I will save $5,000 for a car in 12 months by setting aside $417 each month." This goal is specific (saving for a car), measurable (the amount), achievable (based on your budget), relevant (it aligns with your needs), and time-bound (12 months).

A compelling example is how the famed athlete Michael Phelps approached his goals. From a young age, he set specific targets for his swimming career—countless hours spent in the pool with clear milestones for each event. His commitment to these SMART goals led him to become the most decorated Olympian of all time. Just like Phelps, when you set clear intentions, you establish a path toward your desired outcomes.

2. Prioritizing Short-Term vs. Long-Term Objectives: The Balancing Act

In the jungle, animals must constantly balance their immediate needs with long-term survival. The elephant knows it must find food and water daily, but it also understands the importance of migrating to a safer habitat during droughts. It's a delicate dance of priorities that ensures both short-term sustenance and long-term health.

In your financial life, recognizing the difference between short-term and long-term objectives is vital. Short-term goals, like paying off a credit card or saving for a vacation, provide immediate satisfaction and relieve stress. Long-term goals, such as saving for retirement or purchasing a home, require a more sustained effort and patience.

Consider the story of Sara Blakely, the founder of Spanx. Early in her entrepreneurial journey, she set a short-term goal to sell her product to local stores while also keeping her long-term vision in sight—to create a global brand. By juggling both types of objectives, she built Spanx into a billion-dollar empire. By understanding when to focus on short-term wins and when to invest in long-term growth, she paved her way to success.

3. Identifying Your "Why" Behind Financial Success: The Motivation to Thrive

Every animal in the jungle has a reason for its actions. The mother zebra grazes to provide for her young, while the lion hunts not just for sustenance but to secure its position in the pride. Understanding the "why" behind their behaviours is what drives their daily actions and long-term survival.

In your financial journey, identifying your "why" is crucial. It's the emotional anchor that keeps you motivated, even when the going gets tough. Do you want to buy a home for your family? Save for your children's education? Retire comfortably? Your "why" fuels your ambition and shapes your goals.

Take the example of Tony Robbins, a renowned motivational speaker and author. His "why" stems from a desire to help others achieve their dreams. This deep-seated motivation has driven him to create numerous programs that empower individuals to take control of their finances and lives. By connecting with his "why," Robbins not only inspires others but also sustains his passion and purpose.

Taking the First Step: Building a Foundation

As the jungle awakens with the first rays of sunlight, energy surges through the air. Animals shake off the remnants of sleep, stretch their limbs, and prepare to embrace the day ahead. This moment of awakening isn't just a routine; it's the catalyst for action. In your financial life, taking the first step is crucial to creating momentum and building a strong foundation for the future.

1. Starting an Emergency Fund or Savings: Your Financial Safety Net

In the wild, the unpredictable nature of the jungle means that safety and survival often hinge on being prepared for the unexpected. The resilient meerkat, for example, digs out a burrow to shelter its family from the lurking dangers that may strike at any moment. This instinct for preparation is essential for survival.

Similarly, starting an emergency fund is your financial safety net. It's your buffer against life's surprises—a job loss, an unexpected medical expense, or a sudden home repair. Imagine setting aside a small portion of your income each month until you build up at least three to six months' worth of living expenses. This fund gives you the peace of mind to navigate financial storms, allowing you to face challenges with confidence.

Take the inspiring story of J.K. Rowling. Before she became a bestselling author, Rowling faced dire financial straits as a single mother living on government assistance. She managed to save enough to cushion her transition into her new career by creating an emergency fund. This safety net allowed her to focus on writing without the constant worry of financial instability. Just like the meerkat prepares for danger, you too can build a safety net that empowers you to take risks and pursue your goals.

2. Basic Budgeting Strategies: Charting Your Course

With the sun now fully risen, the jungle thrives as animals set off on their daily quests. The savvy creatures know where to find food, water, and shelter because they've learned to navigate their environment. They understand the importance of having a clear plan.

In your financial life, budgeting serves as your map, guiding you through your spending and helping you allocate resources wisely. Start by tracking your income and expenses for a month. This simple step reveals where your money is going and helps you identify areas to cut back. Then, create a budget that outlines your fixed expenses, variable costs, and savings goals.

A powerful example is how the famous personal finance expert Dave Ramsey advocates for a zero-based budget. This method ensures that every dollar you earn is assigned a purpose, whether for bills, savings, or discretionary spending. By following this strategy, many individuals have taken control of their finances, paid off debt, and built wealth. Just like the animals in the jungle, knowing your financial landscape helps you thrive instead of just surviving.

3. Eliminating Financial Distractions and Preparing for Opportunities: The Art of Focus

As the jungle hums with activity, distractions abound. The rustle of leaves can signal danger, and the sound of a flowing stream can lead an animal astray from its path. To succeed, creatures must remain focused on their goals, tuning out the distractions that threaten their survival.

In your financial life, eliminating distractions is equally crucial. The modern world is rife with temptations—impulse buys, social media, and peer pressure can easily divert you from your financial goals. Recognize what distracts you, whether it's frequent online shopping or extravagant nights out, and set boundaries to regain control.

Consider the story of Tim Ferriss, author of "The 4-Hour Workweek." Ferriss found success by prioritizing what truly mattered, eliminating distractions, and focusing on the opportunities that aligned with his goals. He embraced the concept of "essentialism," where he intentionally chose how to spend his time and resources, allowing him to create a life that aligns with his aspirations.

To prepare for opportunities, stay disciplined and proactive. By maintaining your focus, you'll be ready to seize the right moment when it arises—whether it's a job opportunity, an investment, or a chance to start a side business.

The Dawn of Action

As the sun bathes the jungle in its warm embrace, each animal moves with purpose and intention, embracing the day ahead. By taking actionable steps—starting an emergency fund, implementing budgeting strategies, and eliminating distractions—you build a strong foundation for your financial future.

Just as the jungle comes alive with possibilities, your financial journey begins to flourish when you take that first step. The dawn has awakened your awareness, ignited your intentions, and now it's time to act. With each decision, you shape your future, moving toward the life you envision.

So, as the day unfolds, ask yourself: Are you ready to embrace the momentum and take charge of your financial destiny? The first step is yours to take make it count.

Conclusion: Embracing the Dawn of Financial Awakening

As the day in the jungle unfolds, the vibrant energy of life emerges. The sun, once a mere glimmer on the horizon, has transformed into a powerful force illuminating the path ahead. Just as the jungle awakens with possibilities, your financial journey begins anew with each sunrise—a fresh start filled with hope, intention, and action.

In this chapter, we've explored the profound significance of the sunrise, drawing parallels between the natural world and your financial awakening. The morning light represents not just a new day but a powerful moment of awareness—a time to assess your current financial landscape, to recognize the opportunities that lie before you, and to prepare for the challenges ahead.

We began by highlighting the importance of **awakening awareness**, where you conducted a thorough financial self-assessment, learned to understand your assets and liabilities, and recognized your spending habits. This essential reflection allows you to see the terrain you're navigating, empowering you to make informed decisions as you move forward.

Then we delved into **setting intentions**—defining clear and meaningful financial goals. Much like the creatures of the jungle that prepare for the day with purpose, you learned to set SMART goals, prioritize short- and long-term objectives, and identify your "why." Understanding your motivations fuels your determination, driving you to transform your dreams into actionable plans.

Finally, we explored **taking the first step** towards building a solid foundation. Just as the jungle springs to life with momentum and purpose, you can create your own momentum by starting an emergency fund, implementing effective budgeting strategies, and eliminating financial distractions. Each of these actions contributes to your financial well-being and prepares you for the opportunities that lie ahead.

As the sun climbs higher in the sky, remember that every new day offers a chance to rewrite your financial narrative. Just as the jungle thrives through its cycles of awakening, growth, and adaptation, so too can you evolve your financial life. Embrace the dawn, take control of your intentions, and step boldly into the journey that awaits.

The sunrise symbolizes hope, clarity, and the power of transformation. It is your reminder that every financial decision, every moment of reflection, and every goal you set brings you closer to the financial freedom you desire. So, rise with the sun and let its light guide you toward a future filled with possibilities.

Chapter 2: Antelope, Wildebeests, and Zebras – The Power of Collective Movement

Cue the soft light of dawn breaking across the African plains. The camera pans over a sprawling savannah where the air is filled with the distant thunder of hooves.

Narrator: "*In the heart of the wild, where survival is not just a daily challenge but a way of life, a remarkable event takes place—a symphony of movement that stretches as far as the eye can see. Here, in the vast savannah, the antelopes, wildebeests, and zebras gather by the thousands. Their shared instinct drives them forward, a powerful collective force that traverses endless miles in search of greener pastures and safety from predators lurking in the shadows.*"

The camera zooms in on a herd of antelopes, their sleek bodies poised for action, eyes scanning the horizon for danger.

Narrator: "*The antelope—swift, agile, and ever-watchful. They know that survival demands vigilance. With their sharp instincts, they remind us of the need to stay alert, to anticipate change, and to act quickly when opportunities arise.*"

The scene shifts to wildebeests, trudging across the landscape in seemingly endless streams, their sheer numbers a testament to endurance.

Narrator: "*Then, there are the wildebeests—creatures of endurance and persistence. Through thick and thin, they push forward, their journey a long-term investment in survival. No storm or hardship can break their spirit, as they symbolize the power of resilience in the face of adversity. They show us that success isn't always about speed but about staying the course."*

The camera moves to a herd of zebras, their bold stripes standing out against the golden grass.

Narrator: *"And the zebras—their unique stripes make them stand out, yet their strength lies in numbers. They protect each other from predators, knowing that survival in the wild is a shared effort. Their boldness teaches us to recognize our own distinct value while understanding the power of community, reminding us that standing out and staying together is key to overcoming threats."*

The herds move together, the dust rising in clouds behind them as they march toward their destination.

Narrator: *"These animals, so different yet so intertwined, show us that in the jungle, much like in life, survival is about strategy, unity, and knowing when to act. The great migrations of the African plains are more than a fight for survival; they are a powerful metaphor for financial growth. Whether it's investing wisely, adapting to change, or finding strength in collaboration, success requires us to move with purpose, to learn from the world around us, and to take bold steps toward our goals."*

The camera fades into the horizon as the herd continues its journey.

Narrator: *"In this chapter, we explore how the principles of collective movement and strategy can transform your financial journey. The lessons of the antelope, wildebeests, and zebras teach us that thriving, much like migrating, is not a solo endeavour it's about being part of something bigger, aligning with the right opportunities, and knowing when to run with the herd or stand out on your own."*

Cue the final shot of the sun setting, casting a golden glow over the savannah.

Narrator: *"The journey is long, but with the wisdom of the herd, the destination becomes achievable. The question is: Are you ready to run with the pack?"*

If you're a fan of wildlife documentaries, I'm willing to bet David Attenborough's voice played in your head as you read that earlier scene. His calm yet powerful narration always manages to make the wild feel even more alive. But let me ask you something: Imagine you wake up tomorrow morning, and suddenly, you find yourself in the jungle. Not as a spectator this time, but as the lion—the king of beasts. Can you see yourself chasing down and catching that big, powerful buffalo? It's no easy feat, even for the lion.

Now, let's change that image. Suppose you wake up and find yourself in the jungle, but this time, you're not the lion. Instead, you're an antelope, a wildebeest, or a zebra. You're standing amid that vast savannah, surrounded by ruthless predators, all of them hungry and looking for their next meal. Can you see yourself surviving? Can you imagine outrunning the fastest animal in the world—the cheetah—when it locks onto you as its target?

These scenarios aren't just thrilling wildlife dramas; they're reflections of real-world challenges we face every day. Financially, many of us wake up feeling like the antelope, wildebeest, or zebra—surrounded by risks, unsure how to navigate the dangerous terrain of the market, investments, or even day-to-day money management. The odds can feel stacked against us, like being hunted by a cheetah that's faster, more experienced, and always one step ahead.

But here's the thing: survival in the jungle doesn't depend on raw power or speed alone. It's about strategy, understanding the environment, and moving in alignment with others. The animals we'll discuss in this chapter—the antelope, the wildebeest, and the zebra—each possess their own unique strengths. And those strengths, when understood and applied correctly, make them formidable in the face of even the most relentless predators.

Much like these animals, thriving financially doesn't mean being the strongest or the fastest. It's about understanding your environment, making strategic decisions, and knowing when to rely on others for support. It's about aligning with the right opportunities, navigating risks, and playing to your strengths. In this chapter, we'll explore how the lessons from these herds can be applied to your financial journey. Just like the antelope, wildebeests, and zebras survive through instinct, strategy, and collective effort, you too can find your way through the financial wilderness—if you understand how to move and adapt.

STRENGTH IN NUMBERS: Surviving Through Collective Effort

In the wild, isolation can be a death sentence. But for the antelope, wildebeest, and zebra, survival is rooted in unity. When faced with the looming threat of predators, these animals instinctively band together, creating a powerful defence that even the most fearsome hunters struggle to penetrate. Everyone may be vulnerable on its own, but as a collective, they become an imposing force—a moving wall of strength that's difficult to single out or overwhelm.

In the same way, financial security and growth are often most effectively achieved through collective effort. The idea of "strength in numbers" isn't just a survival tactic in the wild—it's a cornerstone of financial strategy. Whether you're an individual looking to safeguard your wealth or a business navigating uncertain markets, joining forces with others can provide you with an added layer of protection, opportunity, and resilience.

In the financial world, this principal manifests in several ways. **Risk-sharing**, for instance, is a key benefit of pooling resources. When you invest alongside others, whether through partnerships, collective investments, or peer support networks, the risk doesn't rest solely on your shoulders. Just like a herd protects the weaker members by spreading out the danger, financial alliances help you distribute potential losses, ensuring that no single participant bears the full brunt of a market downturn.

Let's take collective investments as an example. Mutual funds, index funds, and crowdfunding initiatives all capitalize on the power of group participation. Investors pool their resources, which allows them to access opportunities that might be out of reach individually. More importantly, this collective approach enables diversification—an essential strategy for minimizing risk. Much like how a predator finds it difficult to focus on one target in a sea of moving bodies, financial risks are spread out and diluted within a diversified investment pool.

Peer support networks also offer critical lifelines, especially during times of financial crisis or instability. In the same way that zebras stand together to confuse and deter predators, individuals and businesses can lean on trusted networks to gain insights, share resources, and weather financial storms. Whether it's informal support among friends or structured groups like investment clubs and business coalitions, these networks provide a sense of security and shared wisdom that can help you navigate rough patches.

Consider how companies form **alliances and partnerships** to grow stronger in competitive markets. In much the same way that wildebeests migrate in vast numbers to find resources and protection, businesses collaborate to share expertise, reduce operational costs, and expand their reach. These strategic alliances often lead to more innovative solutions and greater market strength than going it alone.

Even on an individual level, applying the lesson of collective effort can yield significant results. Group savings schemes, investment cooperatives, and community-based lending circles offer ways to pool financial resources, providing members access to capital they might not be able to gather on their own. For example, in many parts of the world there's informal savings groups which allow participants to save money together and take turns accessing a lump sum. This method has helped countless individuals reach financial goals more quickly and efficiently by drawing on the power of community.

Ultimately, the lesson from the antelope, wildebeests, and zebras is clear: survival—and success—is far easier when you're not alone. In the financial jungle, strength truly lies in numbers. By pooling resources, sharing risks, and working collectively, you can not only survive challenging circumstances but thrive within them.

The Power of Synergy: Complementary Strengths in Action

In the heart of the savannah, a remarkable sight unfolds as antelopes, wildebeests, and zebras move together as one. Despite being distinct species, with their own unique strengths and weaknesses, these animals recognize the power of traveling side by side. They understand that survival doesn't depend solely on their individual capabilities, but on their ability to combine those strengths into a unified force. Together, they create a living, breathing example of synergy—a reminder that collaboration is often the key to overcoming the harshest challenges.

In the financial world, the power of synergy is just as crucial. Much like these animals, people and businesses don't need to navigate their financial landscapes alone. By joining forces with others who have complementary strengths, they can achieve far more together than they could ever accomplish on their own.

Collaboration and partnerships are essential for creating this kind of synergy. Let's take a closer look at how the antelope, wildebeests, and zebras demonstrate this. The antelope's greatest strength is its speed and vigilance. They are often the first to sense danger, alerting the others with their quick reflexes and sharp eyesight. Wildebeests, on the other hand, are known for their endurance and resilience, making them the marathon runners of the group—steady and persistent in their movements. Zebras, with their distinctive stripes, serve as a form of visual protection and confusion for predators. When these three species come together, they complement each other perfectly: the antelope's awareness, the wildebeest's endurance, and the zebra's defence all combine to form a stronger, more capable unit.

In the same way, successful financial ventures often involve **combining different skill sets** or resources to achieve mutual success. Think of a partnership between a tech company and a financial services firm. The tech company might excel in innovation and product development, while the financial firm brings expertise in managing resources and navigating regulations. Separately, each business has its own strengths, but together, they can create a more comprehensive, efficient, and powerful operation.

This concept is echoed in **diversifying strategies**. By working together with others who have different perspectives, skill sets, or resources, you open yourself up to new opportunities and solutions. In investing, for instance, having a diversified portfolio—stocks, bonds, real estate—means you're not relying on one source of growth. Instead, like the animals in the savannah, you're utilizing different strengths to build a stable, more resilient financial foundation.

Consider how **complementary strengths** play out in professional relationships as well. In a business context, an entrepreneur who excels at creative vision might partner with someone who has strong financial acumen. Just as the zebras rely on the antelopes to detect danger, the creative entrepreneur can rely on their financially minded partner to guide the business toward sound investments and long-term growth. By combining their unique talents, they form a partnership that's not only balanced but primed for success.

In the world of finance, synergy can also manifest in **cross-industry collaborations**. For example, when retail companies' partner with logistics firms, they leverage each other's strengths to streamline supply chains, reduce costs, and improve customer service. Much like the zebra, antelope, and wildebeest traveling together for mutual benefit, these businesses can achieve far more through cooperation than they would if they operated in isolation.

There's also an undeniable strength in **diversified perspectives**. When diverse skill sets come together, creative problem-solving is often the result. Take a marketing firm that joins forces with a data analytics company. The marketers bring storytelling, branding, and outreach strategies, while the analytics team provides detailed insights and data-driven decision-making. Together, they create a powerful, holistic approach that neither could achieve alone.

Ultimately, the lesson from these animals is that synergy—built on collaboration, mutual respect, and complementary strengths—creates resilience. Whether in business or personal finance, working with others who bring something different to the table can unlock greater success and security. The wilderness of finance, like the jungle, is unpredictable, but with the right allies and a willingness to collaborate, you can create a system where everyone thrives.

Navigating Together: The Efficiency of Collective Movement

Every year, one of nature's greatest spectacles unfolds across the vast plains of East Africa—the migration of millions of wildebeests, zebras, and antelopes from the Serengeti in Tanzania to the Maasai Mara in Kenya. These animals move in a synchronized flow, covering over 1,800 miles in search of fresh grazing lands and water. It's a journey fraught with peril, from predators lying in wait to treacherous river crossings. Yet, despite the dangers, they follow a time-tested pattern, one that maximizes their chances of survival. Their collective movement ensures they find the resources they need and evade threats that would be too overwhelming to face alone.

In much the same way, financial success often hinges on knowing when—and how—to move. Just as these animals migrate together in search of greener pastures, investors and businesses must be attuned to **market trends** and opportunities that require strategic shifts. Whether it's moving capital to emerging markets, pivoting business models to meet changing consumer demands, or shifting investments in response to economic downturns, those who navigate together with others stand a far better chance of surviving and thriving.

Take the **Great Migration** from the Serengeti to the Maasai Mara as a perfect example. Millions of wildebeests and their companions don't make this gruelling journey alone; they move together. The zebras, with their exceptional memory for migration routes, lead the way, while the wildebeests, guided by their instincts and sheer numbers, follow in mass. Antelopes, with their keen senses, add another layer of protection. Their synchronized movement allows them to outmanoeuvre predators, cross rivers teeming with crocodiles, and reach lush grazing lands that ensure their survival. Each animal plays its part, and through their collective movement, they find safety and new opportunities.

In the financial world, **collective market shifts** operate in much the same way. Investors often look to industry leaders, expert advisors, and economic signals to guide their movements. Following smart investments or responding to **market trends** can be a game-changer, allowing you to get ahead of market shifts before they happen. Just like the migration, where early movers tend to find the best resources, businesses and individuals who adapt quickly to market changes can secure new opportunities before others catch on.

Consider how businesses strategically **pivot** when the market landscape changes. During economic downturns or periods of technological disruption, companies often need to adjust their approach. Much like how animals instinctively know it's time to move when the dry season hits the Serengeti, businesses often find themselves needing to shift their focus. Those that successfully pivot—whether by transitioning to digital platforms, exploring new geographic markets, or changing product lines—are often the ones that survive and prosper. Blockbuster companies like Netflix, which transitioned from DVD rentals to online streaming, or Amazon's pivot from a bookstore to a global e-commerce empire, demonstrate how critical it is to **move in sync with changing market conditions.**

The importance of **following market leaders** mirrors the wildebeest's reliance on the zebra's knowledge during migration. When industry leaders make bold moves—whether by shifting capital to promising sectors, expanding into new regions, or adopting new technologies—they often set off a chain reaction, as smaller players follow their lead. The herd mentality in finance isn't just about blindly following the pack, though. It's about recognizing when **smart investments** or strategies are gaining traction and aligning your actions accordingly.

Another powerful example of collective movement in finance is the rise of **investment shifts** in response to global trends. For instance, in recent years, there has been a surge of investment toward green energy and technology companies as the world becomes more focused on sustainability. Investors collectively moving towards these sectors are not only benefiting from the potential for growth but are also positioning themselves to avoid the long-term risks associated with traditional energy sources. In essence, they're mirroring the migratory animals—seeking out new, fertile ground while avoiding landscapes that are drying up.

Ultimately, the wildebeests, zebras, and antelopes don't make their journey by chance. Their movement is strategic, synchronized, and driven by necessity. In the same way, businesses and individuals who understand the importance of **strategic**

pivots and collective movement are better positioned to adapt to changes, take advantage of new opportunities, and avoid the dangers of stagnation. Just as animals rely on their instincts and each other to survive in the wild, savvy investors and businesses rely on market insights, collaboration, and well-timed action to stay ahead of the curve in the financial jungle.

Leadership Within the Herd: Guiding the Collective

In the sprawling savannah, herds of wildebeests, zebras, and antelopes move in perfect harmony, but make no mistake—their collective strength relies on leadership. While the majority of the herd follows, certain animals take on the responsibility of guiding the group, deciding when to move, where to find resources, and how to avoid danger. These leaders, often the most experienced or sharp-eyed, understand that one wrong decision could spell disaster for the entire herd. In a landscape where life and death hinge on each movement, effective leadership is not just a position—it's a survival skill.

In the financial world, leadership operates much the same way. **Financial leadership** is about guiding teams, organizations, or even communities through the ever-shifting markets, making decisions that ensure collective success and stability. Just as herds look to their leaders for direction, employees, investors, and partners turn to those with vision and expertise to navigate through challenging economic landscapes.

Let's take the example of a zebra herd. Zebras are known to follow certain individuals who have a heightened awareness of the environment—those who know when danger is near or when it's time to move toward greener pastures. The leaders don't always act out of personal gain; they move with the herd's best interest in mind. In this way, they provide **vision** and foresight, helping the group thrive. Similarly, strong financial leaders are those who look beyond immediate gains to secure the long-term prosperity of their team or organization. They identify market trends, anticipate risks, and strategically guide their companies toward stability and growth.

Effective leadership requires more than just being in front—it involves making **strategic decisions** that safeguard and propel the collective forward. In business, this means that a great leader must possess a deep understanding of the financial landscape, much like the herd leaders understand the shifting environment. Visionary CEOs like Tim Cook at Apple or Mary Barra at General Motors are perfect examples. They lead not only with their expertise but also with the ability to guide their companies through innovation and market shifts. They see around corners, positioning their organizations to capitalize on new opportunities and avoid pitfalls that could jeopardize long-term success.

Guiding teams through market challenges is where leadership shines the brightest. Just as a wildebeest leader instinctively knows when to cross a river despite the lurking crocodiles, financial leaders must make bold moves during uncertain times. In turbulent markets, they keep the collective calm and focused, ensuring that fear doesn't dictate decisions. For example, during economic recessions, strong leaders maintain a clear focus on long-term goals, while reassuring employees, partners, and investors that the company's direction remains solid. Warren Buffett, known for his measured approach during times of market volatility, embodies this type of steady leadership. His famous mantra of being "fearful when others are greedy and greedy when others are fearful" reflects the kind of calm yet decisive leadership that inspires confidence in followers.

Leaders also serve as the **beacon of trust** within the financial herd. Much like animals trust their leaders to guide them through dangerous terrain, teams rely on their financial leaders to provide clarity and security. This trust is built through consistent, sound decision-making, and the ability to communicate effectively during both prosperous and challenging times. It's about fostering a sense of unity and shared purpose—ensuring that everyone, from the top executives to the newest team members, understands and buys into the vision.

Consider how **leadership within communities** can drive collective success. In smaller financial ecosystems, such as startup hubs or local business alliances, strong leadership can mean the difference between growth and stagnation. Leaders in these environments often function much like the elder animals in the herd—offering guidance based on experience, creating strategies to adapt to shifting market conditions, and helping others rise by providing mentorship and resources. By fostering collaboration and guiding the community with vision and decisiveness, these leaders ensure that the whole collective thrives, much like how a herd's survival depends on the wisdom of its guides.

Ultimately, leadership within the herd is about **responsibility**—the responsibility to guide, protect, and uplift those who rely on you. In both the wild and the financial world, success doesn't just happen by chance. It's the product of strategic, informed leadership that understands when to take risks, when to hold back, and when to rally the collective. Whether you're leading a team, a company, or an investment group, the lesson from the animal kingdom is clear: effective leadership is the key to guiding the collective toward long-term success and prosperity.

The Harsh Truth: Success vs. Failure in Life's Jungle

In the wild, life is a continuous struggle for survival. Each day brings challenges that test the resilience and strength of its inhabitants. As the sun rises, a young gazelle takes its first steps, instinctively aware that its life hangs by a thread. With predators lurking in the shadows, the odds are stacked against it. While some animals thrive and adapt, surviving for years, others, like that newborn gazelle, may not make it past their first hours. The harsh reality is that in nature, success is never guaranteed; it is a complex interplay of timing, preparedness, collaboration, and, yes, even luck.

Similarly, in the financial jungle, the landscape is fraught with uncertainties. Despite diligent efforts and strategic planning, some individuals achieve remarkable success, while others, despite their hard work, may find themselves facing failure. Just as in the wild, the outcomes are often unpredictable. The question looms large: Why do some thrive while others falter, even when they seem equally committed?

Timing is one of the most critical factors in this equation. In the jungle, the difference between life and death can come down to the precise moment an animal decides to flee or feed. Those who capitalize on the right opportunities at the right time are often the ones who survive and thrive. In the financial world, timing can make or break an investment. A savvy investor who buys into a trending market before it peaks can reap enormous rewards, while another who enters too late may incur significant losses.

Preparedness also plays a pivotal role. In the wild, animals that can adapt to their surroundings and learn from past experiences are more likely to succeed. Consider the resilient meerkats that watch over their young and work together to alert each other to danger. Their success lies in their constant vigilance and preparedness for threats. Similarly, individuals who equip themselves with knowledge, skills, and resources are better positioned to seize opportunities. Those who invest in continuous learning and stay informed about market trends often navigate the financial landscape more successfully than their less-prepared counterparts.

Collaboration is another essential element of survival. Just as animals form alliances and herds to fend off predators, individuals and businesses must recognize the power of collective effort. Partnerships can amplify strengths and provide a safety net during tough times. In the financial realm, collaborative networks, such as mentorships or investment groups, can significantly enhance one's chances of success. By sharing knowledge and resources, these networks foster an environment where everyone can thrive, mirroring how animals rely on one another for protection and survival in the jungle.

However, even with the best strategies and collaborations, **luck** remains an unpredictable variable. In nature, fortune often favours the bold. A sudden storm might drive food sources to unexpected locations, giving some animals a bounty while others starve. In finance, luck can manifest in various forms: a market crash that wipes out investments, or a chance encounter leading to a lucrative partnership. While hard work and strategy lay the groundwork for success, embracing the unpredictable nature of opportunity is crucial. Recognizing that not everything is within your control allows you to adapt and pivot when circumstances change.

Ultimately, understanding the **unpredictable nature of opportunity** equips you to navigate your own journey through life's jungle. Acknowledging that success is influenced by timing, preparedness, collaboration, and luck fosters resilience. Just like in the wild, where animals learn to adapt and evolve, those in the financial world must remain agile, ready to shift strategies and embrace new opportunities as they arise.

The harsh truth is that while we may strive for success, we must also be prepared to face setbacks and failures. Embracing the complexity of this reality empowers us to learn from our experiences, harness our strengths, and build a network of support that will help us navigate the unpredictable paths of our financial journeys. In the end, it's not just about survival—it's about thriving amidst the challenges, much like the resilient creatures of the jungle.

Embracing the Collective Journey

As we navigate through the vibrant tapestry of life in the jungle, the stories of antelope, wildebeests, and zebras remind us of the profound lessons that nature teaches us about survival and success. In this chapter, we've explored the importance of **collective effort** in overcoming challenges. Just as these herbivores band together for safety, we, too, can find strength in numbers, collaborating with others to share risks and resources in our financial journeys.

We've delved into the **power of synergy**, where the unique strengths of different species enhance their chances of survival. This serves as a powerful metaphor for the business world, where diverse skill sets and partnerships can lead to greater achievements. By recognizing and leveraging each other's strengths, we create a dynamic environment ripe for innovation and success.

Moreover, the migratory patterns of these animals showcase the **efficiency of collective movement**. Their synchronized strategies in seeking resources and avoiding dangers mirror the strategic financial pivots individuals and businesses must make in a constantly changing landscape. Understanding market trends and collectively adjusting our strategies can open new opportunities and help us navigate the complexities of the financial jungle.

In examining **leadership within the herd**, we've seen how strong, visionary leaders guide their communities through uncertainty. Just as a wise zebra leads its herd to greener pastures, effective financial leadership inspires trust and fosters collaboration, ensuring the collective can weather storms and seize opportunities together.

Finally, we confronted **the harsh truth of success and failure**. In both the wild and the financial world, outcomes are not guaranteed. Timing, preparedness, collaboration, and luck all play critical roles in determining our paths. Embracing this reality enables us to remain resilient, adapt to challenges, and learn from our experiences, empowering us to navigate our financial journeys with confidence.

As we conclude this chapter, let us carry forward the wisdom gleaned from the jungle. Just like the antelope, wildebeests, and zebras that thrive through cooperation and strategy, we, too, can harness the power of collective effort and smart leadership. By working together, sharing knowledge, and supporting one another, we can create a robust foundation for success, ready to embrace the unpredictable adventures that lie ahead in our own financial jungles.

Chapter Three: Droughts

In the wild, the arrival of a drought is not announced with a roar or a sudden storm. It creeps in slowly, like a shadow stretching across the savanna. The waterholes dry up, the lush grasses wither, and the once-thriving herds of animals are forced to make difficult choices. Some will travel hundreds of miles in search of better grazing grounds, while others remain and face the relentless heat, hoping to survive until the rains return. For every creature, from the smallest insect to the mighty elephant, the drought is a test—a battle against scarcity and uncertainty.

Just as the animals in the jungle endure these harsh seasons, financial droughts are inevitable in our own lives. There will be times when the economic landscape shifts, opportunities dwindle, and resources grow scarce. It might be a personal financial crisis, a recession, or a business slowdown. Like the wildebeests that gather at a shrinking waterhole, we must find ways to endure these tough periods, navigating the drought with patience, strategy, and foresight.

But in every drought, there are lessons to be learned. The animals that survive are not just the strongest, but the smartest—those that know how to conserve, adapt, and seize opportunities even when they seem few and far between. In the financial world, the same is true. Thriving during lean times requires understanding your resources, knowing when to make bold moves, and when to hold back. It's about resilience and adaptability, traits that can determine whether you emerge stronger when the drought breaks or if you are left behind, weakened by the harsh conditions.

As we delve into this chapter, we will explore how to prepare for financial droughts, how to weather them, and, most importantly, how to use them as opportunities for growth and renewal. Just like the survivors of the jungle, those who endure financial hardships often come out stronger, wiser, and more equipped to face the future.

Enduring Scarcity: Managing Financial Droughts

As the scorching sun beats down on the savanna, the landscape begins to change dramatically. Waterholes, once teeming with life, shrink until they are mere puddles, while the vibrant green grass turns to brittle brown. For the animals that call this harsh environment home, survival hinges on resilience and resourcefulness. In this moment of scarcity, herds that once roamed freely huddle around the last remaining water sources, their movements deliberate and calculated. Each decision is made with the goal of endurance—prioritizing essentials overindulgences becomes second nature.

The financial world mirrors this struggle. Just as drought affects the animals, periods of financial scarcity can hit individuals and businesses unexpectedly. An economic downturn, a sudden job loss, or a personal crisis can dry up income streams, forcing you to adapt quickly. In these times, survival instincts kick in, prompting you to conserve resources and manage with what you have on hand.

To weather the storm of financial drought, the first step is to trim unnecessary expenses. Think of how a lion carefully saves its energy, avoiding futile hunts when prey is scarce. Similarly, it's time to examine your finances closely and identify areas where resources are being squandered. Non-essential spending—luxuries and entertainment—must be curtailed. This is the moment to refine your budget, zeroing in on what truly matters: food, shelter, utilities, and the essential costs that support your everyday life. Like an animal shedding non-vital activities to conserve energy, you too must let go of discretionary spending that depletes your reserves.

Building and maintaining essential reserves is equally important. During droughts, animals often rely on hidden water sources and any stored energy they have to survive. In your financial landscape, this means having an emergency fund to tap into when income slows or expenses rise. Ideally, this reserve should be established before the drought hits, but if you're already facing financial scarcity, your focus should shift to conserving what you have. Use your reserves wisely, ensuring they last as long as possible by stretching them for essential needs.

When resources are limited, prioritizing needs over wants becomes a vital survival tactic. Animals facing scarcity don't chase after unnecessary goals; they focus on what's essential for survival. In times of financial drought, your focus should similarly shift to sustaining the basics: paying bills, maintaining a roof over your head, and ensuring your fundamental needs are met. Just as a wildebeest wisely chooses to rest rather than run when water is scarce, financial survival means resisting the temptation to make unnecessary purchases or engage in risky ventures.

Navigating through financial droughts calls for a resilient mindset. It's crucial to recognize that this challenging period is temporary, but only if you play your cards wisely. Conserve your financial energy, make strategic decisions, and avoid panic. The most successful individuals and businesses aren't those who never face adversity; they are the ones who adapt, shed excess burdens, and endure until the landscape shifts back in their favour.

ADAPTING TO HARSH CONDITIONS: Thriving in Tough Markets

When drought descends upon the savanna, the struggle for survival becomes palpable. The once vibrant landscape is transformed into a canvas of browns and yellows, forcing every creature to rethink its approach to life. Some animals begin to adapt instinctively. As the sun sets, they emerge from their shaded shelters, taking advantage of the cooler temperatures to forage for food. This innate ability to adjust is crucial, not just for survival but for thriving against the odds.

Consider the bustling city during an economic downturn, where businesses, much like those animals, must adapt to new realities. Restaurants that thrived on foot traffic suddenly find themselves empty as customers stay home. The savvy ones pivot quickly, embracing takeout and delivery options. Shake Shack, for instance, rapidly shifted its operations to focus on drive-thru services and outdoor dining, discovering new ways to keep customers satisfied and sales flowing.

Flexibility is key in these turbulent times. Think of a skilled artisan who creates beautiful, handcrafted jewellery. When the pandemic hits and sales slump, instead of waiting for things to return to normal, this artisan explores new markets. They dive into e-commerce, showcasing their creations online. By utilizing social media and digital marketing strategies, they connect with a broader audience, finding opportunities that didn't exist before.

This adaptability not only preserves their business but also opens new revenue streams.

Investors, too, must navigate these changing waters. Picture a financial strategist observing market fluctuations. Instead of clinging to a single asset class, they diversify their portfolio—spreading investments across stocks, bonds, and even real estate. During the 2008 financial crisis, those who took this approach weathered the storm better than those who concentrated their efforts in one area. Flexibility in financial strategies can transform challenges into opportunities for growth.

Retraining and upskilling can also be game changers. A bartender, suddenly out of work, decides to take online courses to learn digital marketing. With newfound knowledge, they find a position within a tech company that's thriving, thanks to the demand for online services. This shift not only provides immediate income but also paves the way for a long-term career in an evolving industry.

Adapting to harsh conditions requires a willingness to embrace change and think creatively. Whether it's adjusting business models, exploring new avenues, or retraining for emerging roles, the ability to pivot can lead to success even in tough markets. As the savanna springs back to life after the drought, those who adapt can thrive, discovering paths they may never have imagined before.

OPPORTUNISTIC PREDATORS: Capitalizing During Financial Droughts

In the heart of the savanna, a lone cheetah lurks in the shadows, keenly observing a herd of antelope. The sun beats down mercilessly, and the animals, feeling the strain of the drought, have grown weaker. Their once-vibrant energy is now sapped, and with every day that passes, they become easier targets. The cheetah, aware of this vulnerability, remains patient, knowing that opportunity often arises in moments of hardship.

In the financial world, much like in the savanna, challenges create unique opportunities for those who are prepared to seize them. Economic downturns can make many investors anxious, leading them to retreat and avoid risks. Yet for those who dare to step forward, these conditions can be incredibly advantageous. When the market dips and prices fall, it becomes a prime time to buy undervalued assets that others may overlook or shy away from.

To take advantage of these financial droughts, you must keep a sharp eye on market trends and conditions. Much like the cheetah that watches its prey for signs of weakness, savvy investors monitor the economic landscape to identify opportunities. For instance, during the pandemic, numerous companies saw their stock prices plummet. While many were quick to sell, a few astute investors recognized the potential for recovery and capitalized on these lower prices, leading to significant profits as the market rebounded.

Being willing to take calculated risks is crucial during times of economic uncertainty. While fear can paralyse many, the successful investor maintains a focus on long-term goals and the potential for growth. Just as the cheetah understands that a successful hunt requires both patience and decisiveness, you too should approach investments with a strategic mindset.

Diversification plays a key role in navigating these challenging times. Just as a predator doesn't rely on one type of prey, having a varied investment portfolio can safeguard against losses in a single sector. By spreading your investments across different assets—stocks, bonds, real estate—you can better position yourself to take advantage of various opportunities as they arise.

Preparation is another essential component. Much like the cheetah that stays in peak physical condition to spring into action when the moment is right, you should ensure you're financially prepared to act when opportunities present themselves. This could involve keeping cash reserves ready for investment or continually educating yourself about potential market shifts. The more prepared you are, the better your chances of success.

In the face of financial droughts, those who can adapt and remain vigilant can turn challenges into opportunities. By embracing calculated risk-taking, staying informed about market conditions, and being ready to seize the moment, you can navigate the unpredictable landscape and thrive. Just like the opportunistic predator in the savanna, you can transform adversity into a pathway to success.

Migration for Survival: Knowing When to Move On

In the captivating tones of David Attenborough, one might hear: "As the sun sets on the dry savanna, herds of wildebeest gather, sensing the urgency of survival. With their instinctive understanding of the land, they begin a long journey towards the distant river, where life still flows. This ancient migration is not just a quest for food and water; it is a testament to resilience, adaptability, and the unyielding will to survive in the face of adversity."

In life, just as in nature, there comes a time when the current circumstances may no longer serve your best interests. Animals like the wildebeest exemplify the importance of recognizing when to migrate in search of sustenance. For individuals navigating their financial journey, this can manifest as knowing when to shift careers, move to a new market, or pivot investment strategies to ensure ongoing growth and stability.

When the resources in your current environment dwindle, it may be time to explore new opportunities. Just as the wildebeest instinctively sense the changing landscape, individuals must remain attuned to their circumstances. This might mean recognizing that a stagnant job is holding you back or that a particular investment strategy isn't yielding the desired returns. Being aware of these signs can help you make informed decisions about your next move.

Career shifts can often be daunting, but like the brave herds forging ahead toward the life-giving waters, embracing change can lead to newfound success. For instance, consider an employee who has spent years in a declining industry. By observing market trends and recognizing the rise of technology, they decide to retrain and transition into a burgeoning field such as cybersecurity or renewable energy. This strategic pivot not only revitalizes their career but also aligns them with a sector poised for growth, much like the wildebeest finding fertile grounds after a long migration.

Investment strategies may also need to adapt in response to changing conditions. If an investor notices that certain assets are underperforming, it could be a signal to reassess their portfolio. Like migrating animals seeking greener pastures, a savvy investor might decide to liquidate stagnant holdings and allocate resources to emerging markets or innovative startups with high growth potential. This ability to pivot is crucial in ensuring long-term financial health.

Moving to new markets is another strategic approach to survival. When one area becomes saturated or inhospitable, seeking new terrain can open doors to unexplored possibilities. Entrepreneurs who recognize the potential in a different geographical area or demographic can position themselves to thrive. Just as the herds follow ancient migratory paths to find new resources, business owners must be willing to venture into unfamiliar territory to secure their future.

In the dance of life, knowing when to move on is a skill that can mean the difference between survival and stagnation. Embracing change, whether through a career shift, strategic investment adjustments, or relocating to new markets, can provide fresh opportunities and growth. Much like the wildebeest embarking on their arduous journey, you too can navigate the challenges and uncertainties of your financial landscape, ensuring that your path remains aligned with your goals. In this way, migration becomes not just a means of survival but a gateway to prosperity.

Preparing for the Drought: Building Resilience Before It Hits

In the vast tapestry of the animal kingdom, survival often hinges on the unique skills and strategies that each species employs. For instance, elephants, known for their remarkable memory and intelligence, can locate hidden water sources even in the harshest droughts. They remember the locations of ancient wells and can navigate great distances to access these vital resources, showcasing their ability to plan. Meanwhile, squirrels have mastered the art of preparation by gathering and storing food in various locations, ensuring they have enough sustenance to weather the lean times. These adaptive behaviours highlight the importance of foresight and preparation in navigating challenges.

Just as these animals build resilience against droughts, individuals can adopt similar strategies to safeguard their financial well-being. The first line of defence is establishing an emergency fund. Much like elephants that recall where to find water, having a savings buffer allows you to access funds when unexpected expenses arise. This fund should ideally cover three to six months' worth of living expenses, providing you with the peace of mind to navigate uncertain times.

Diversifying income streams is another critical strategy to prepare for financial droughts. Just as squirrels gather food from different sources, individuals can explore side gigs or passive income opportunities to create a more stable financial foundation. For instance, someone might consider freelance work, investments in rental properties, or creating an online business. By having multiple income sources, you increase your chances of weathering economic downturns.

Financial planning plays a vital role in resilience. Just as animals instinctively prepare for harsh seasons, individuals must be proactive in managing their finances. This means creating a comprehensive budget that prioritizes savings and essential expenses. Tools such as budgeting apps or financial planners can assist in tracking income and expenses, ensuring that you're always ready for unexpected challenges.

Moreover, risk management is crucial in building resilience. Like animals that assess their environment and make strategic choices to avoid danger, individuals should evaluate their financial risks and take measures to mitigate them. This could involve investing in insurance, understanding market volatility, and diversifying investment portfolios. For instance, an investor might choose to spread their investments across various asset classes—stocks, bonds, and real estate—to shield themselves from market fluctuations.

In conclusion, preparing for financial droughts requires a multifaceted approach that mirrors the adaptive strategies found in the animal kingdom. By establishing emergency funds, diversifying income streams, engaging in proactive financial planning, and managing risks, individuals can cultivate the resilience needed to thrive during challenging times. Just as elephants and squirrels exemplify foresight and adaptability, so too can you strengthen your financial foundation, ensuring that when droughts do arrive, you're ready to face them head-on.

Weathering the Storms of Life's Droughts

Navigating the unpredictable landscape of financial challenges can feel daunting, much like the relentless drought that tests the mettle of even the strongest animals. Yet, just as the wild thrives on resilience, so too can you emerge stronger from your financial trials. Throughout this chapter, we've explored the profound lessons that nature offers, highlighting the necessity of preparation, adaptability, and resourcefulness in the face of adversity.

The essence of thriving during financial droughts lies not only in enduring the hardship but also in seizing the opportunity that often lies hidden within the struggle. Each strategy we've discussed—whether it's managing scarcity, adapting to harsh conditions, or preparing in advance—serves as a testament to the power of resilience. These principles can transform your approach to financial challenges, turning obstacles into stepping stones for growth and prosperity.

As you continue your journey through this book, remember that the path to financial success is rarely linear. It's filled with unexpected twists and turns, much like the wild. By harnessing the lessons learned from nature's tenacity, you can develop a mindset that embraces change and welcomes the opportunities that arise even in the toughest of times.

So, are you ready to step into your own wilderness of financial discovery? Are you prepared to cultivate the resilience and foresight needed to navigate the inevitable droughts life will present? Your journey is just beginning. Embrace the challenges, learn from the strategies of the wild, and watch as you transform your financial landscape into one of abundance and success. Each chapter you delve into brings you closer to mastering your financial destiny, empowering you to thrive no matter the circumstances.

Let the story of your financial journey unfold with the same spirit of resilience that defines the natural world. Join me in this exploration, and together, we will uncover the secrets to flourishing amid life's unpredictable droughts. The adventure awaits—turn the page and let's continue this transformative journey together!

Chapter Four: Hippo

As dawn breaks over the African savanna, the scene transforms into a vibrant tapestry of life. Amid the shimmering waters, a formidable figure emerges the hippo. With its massive body and seemingly laid-back demeanour, this creature is often misunderstood. While it may look like a gentle giant, the hippo is a master of survival, perfectly adapted to its environment.

These colossal mammals spend much of their day submerged in water, seeking refuge from the sweltering sun, their massive mouths only occasionally breaking the surface. When night falls, however, the hippo ventures onto land, revealing its true nature. This is when it forages, traveling considerable distances in search of food and asserting its dominance over territory. The hippo teaches us an essential lesson: that beneath a calm exterior lies a powerful force, ready to defend its own.

In the financial world, the hippo serves as a reminder of the importance of balance—between strength and vulnerability, visibility and discretion. Just as the hippo must navigate its dual existence, individuals must learn to manage the complexities of their financial lives. This chapter will explore how, like the hippo, we can embrace our strengths while staying aware of the dangers that lurk beneath the surface.

Through the lens of the hippo's life, we'll delve into themes of resilience, adaptability, and the fine line between caution and boldness. As we navigate the sometimes-treacherous waters of finance, we'll uncover strategies for finding stability in a world that is anything but predictable. Join us as we embark on a journey through the depths of financial wisdom, inspired by one of nature's most intriguing creatures.

THE STRENGTH OF THE Hippo: Harnessing Inner Resources

Beneath the shimmering surface of a river, the hippo lurks, a formidable presence in its aquatic domain. With a robust body and powerful jaws, it commands respect from other creatures that dare to enter its territory. Hippos don't just rely on their size; they embody a fierce determination that allows them to protect their resources and ensure their survival in the wild. This strength is not just physical; it is a testament to their ability to leverage their unique capabilities to thrive.

In the financial landscape, the lesson is clear: just as hippos harness their immense strength, individuals and businesses must identify and utilize their unique resources to carve out a solid financial foundation. This begins with recognizing your personal strengths those skills and attributes that set you apart. Are you a strategic thinker? Do you possess a talent for negotiation? Perhaps you have a deep understanding of a specific market or industry. By acknowledging these strengths, you can cultivate a more robust financial identity, empowering yourself to navigate challenges with confidence.

Leveraging your core competencies is crucial in establishing a strong financial position. Much like a hippo uses its formidable size to deter predators, you should utilize your expertise to create a competitive advantage. For instance, if you are well-versed in financial analysis, you can make informed investment decisions that optimize returns. If you have a knack for marketing, applying that knowledge can boost your business visibility and attract more clients. It's about using what you already possess to build a resilient financial framework.

Furthermore, understanding the resources at your disposal whether they be financial assets, supportive networks, or knowledge enables you to harness your inner strengths effectively. Like the hippo, which knows how to manoeuvre through water, you too must navigate your financial environment wisely. This may involve seeking mentorship, investing in personal development, or collaborating with others to pool resources for greater impact.

Ultimately, the strength of the hippo serves as a powerful metaphor for financial success. By identifying your unique abilities, leveraging your core competencies, and utilizing your resources, you can create a formidable financial foundation that stands the test of time. Just as the hippo thrives in its territory, so too can you flourish in the world of finance, turning your strengths into a powerful ally on your journey toward prosperity.

ENDURANCE IN THE WATER: Navigating Financial Currents

Imagine a sweltering afternoon on the African savanna, the sun beating down relentlessly. Yet, just below the surface of the water, a hippo remains unfazed, its massive body buoyed by the cool embrace of the river. This creature thrives in its aquatic environment, a testament to the endurance and adaptability required to navigate the challenges of life in the wild. It's a reminder that in the world of finance, just as in nature, the ability to adapt and endure is crucial for survival.

In financial markets, conditions can change rapidly, much like the shifting currents of a river. Unexpected events—economic downturns, shifts in consumer behaviour, or global crises—can create turbulence that threatens financial stability. During these times, resilience becomes paramount. Just as the hippo submerges itself to find refuge from the heat, individuals and businesses must learn to navigate these turbulent waters by remaining adaptable in their financial strategies.

The key to enduring financial currents lies in flexibility. Like the hippo that adjusts its position in the water to maintain stability, you must be prepared to pivot your financial approach as market conditions fluctuate. This might mean diversifying investments, reevaluating budgets, or exploring new revenue streams. For instance, during an economic downturn, businesses may need to innovate their product offerings or adopt cost-cutting measures to maintain profitability. By being proactive and willing to adapt, you can weather the storm and emerge stronger on the other side.

Staying cool under pressure is another vital component of financial endurance. Just as a hippo remains calm amidst the chaos of its environment, maintaining composure during financial challenges allows you to make informed decisions rather than reactive ones. This might involve seeking advice from financial professionals, engaging in strategic planning, or taking the time to reflect on long-term goals instead of being swayed by short-term anxieties.

Moreover, cultivating resilience—an essential trait of the hippo—can empower you to withstand the unpredictable nature of financial markets. This means developing a mindset that embraces challenges as opportunities for growth rather than obstacles to success. Individuals who adopt a resilient attitude are more likely to persevere through tough times, learning valuable lessons along the way that can inform better financial decisions in the future.

Ultimately, the endurance of the hippo serves as an inspiring metaphor for navigating financial currents. By embracing adaptability, remaining cool under pressure, and fostering resilience, you can skilfully manoeuvre through the challenges of the financial landscape. Just as the hippo finds solace in the water, you too can cultivate a strategy that ensures your financial well-being, even in the face of adversity.

The Vulnerable Giant: Recognizing Financial Risks

In the heart of the African wilderness, the hippo reigns as one of the largest and most formidable animals in the water. Its sheer size and strength make it an impressive sight, yet beneath that tough exterior lies a creature acutely aware of its vulnerabilities. Despite its dominance, the hippo must remain vigilant, navigating threats from predators and the challenges of its environment. This paradox of strength and vulnerability offers a powerful lesson in the financial world: recognizing and addressing your financial risks is crucial to safeguarding your future.

Financial vulnerability is often not as visible as a hippo's massive form, yet it exists in various forms for individuals and businesses alike. Debt, poor investment choices, and a lack of diversification can quietly erode financial stability, much like unseen predators lurking at the water's edge. Identifying these risks is the first step toward achieving financial security. Just as hippos are alert to their surroundings, you must cultivate an awareness of your financial landscape, regularly assessing where vulnerabilities lie.

Take, for example, the risk of accumulating excessive debt. Like a hippo submerged in murky waters, it can be easy to overlook how quickly debt can rise. Understanding the terms of your loans and credit, along with their potential impact on your financial health, is essential. By staying informed about interest rates and repayment schedules, you can create a strategy to manage and reduce your debt before it spirals out of control.

Equally important is the recognition of poor investments. In the financial jungle, not every opportunity shines brightly. Much like a hippo's false sense of security when it underestimates its enemies, investing without thorough research can lead to costly mistakes. Conducting a vulnerability assessment of your investment portfolio can illuminate areas that require adjustment or diversification. By evaluating the performance and risk levels of your assets, you can make informed decisions that align with your long-term financial goals.

Proactive risk management is akin to the hippo's instinct to stay aware of its environment. Recognizing potential threats allows you to take preventive measures before they escalate. This might involve developing a robust financial plan that includes emergency funds, insurance policies, and diversified income streams. By creating a safety net, you can cushion the impact of unforeseen events, just as a hippo might retreat to deeper waters when danger approaches.

Awareness of financial risks also means being prepared for environmental changes, whether that's market fluctuations, economic downturns, or shifts in personal circumstances. Just as a hippo must adapt to its changing surroundings to survive, you too must remain flexible in your financial strategies. Regularly reviewing and adjusting your financial plan in response to new information or changing conditions is vital for maintaining stability.

Ultimately, the lesson from the vulnerable giant is clear: recognizing financial risks is not a sign of weakness but a demonstration of wisdom. By identifying vulnerabilities, assessing your financial landscape, and taking proactive measures, you can fortify your financial position against potential threats. Just as the hippo remains vigilant in a world filled with challenges, you can cultivate a resilient mindset that empowers you to navigate the complexities of the financial jungle with confidence.

The Unique Nature of Hippos: Standing Out in the Financial World

In the vast tapestry of the animal kingdom, few creatures are as distinctive as the hippo. With their massive bodies, barrel-shaped torsos, and powerful jaws, hippos are perfectly designed to thrive both in the water and on land. This unique ability to dominate in two environments showcases not only their adaptability but also serves as a powerful metaphor for standing out in the financial world. Just as hippos carve out their space in the savanna and rivers, individuals and businesses must discover and embrace their unique strengths to differentiate themselves in the competitive marketplace.

Differentiation is vital in a crowded financial landscape. Just as the hippo's imposing presence sets it apart from other herbivores, a unique selling proposition (USP) can elevate a brand above its competitors. To begin this journey, you must first understand what makes your offerings distinct. This might involve leveraging your expertise, enhancing customer experiences, or delivering innovative solutions that others don't provide. Just as the hippo's dual capabilities allow it to thrive in various environments, businesses that can adapt their strategies to meet diverse market needs can position themselves for success.

Consider a small business that specializes in eco-friendly products. While many companies may offer similar items, what sets this business apart is its commitment to sustainability and ethical sourcing. By clearly articulating these values and showcasing the story behind each product, this company can attract customers who prioritize eco-conscious choices. In the same way that hippos establish dominance by utilizing their unique traits like their size for protection and their agile movements in water this business can leverage its values and story to build a strong brand identity.

Branding plays a crucial role in standing out. A well-crafted brand not only communicates what you do but also conveys the essence of who you are. Hippos, despite their formidable appearance, often evoke a sense of charm and curiosity. This duality can inspire brands to explore how they present themselves combining strength with approachability. A brand that resonates with its audience is one that embraces authenticity and connects on a deeper level. Think of brands like Apple or Nike, which have carved out unique positions by focusing on innovation and empowerment, respectively. By being true to their identity and values, these brands have built loyal followings.

The ability to dominate both aquatic and terrestrial realms mirrors how businesses can navigate multiple markets or sectors. A company that understands its core strengths and applies them across various platforms can reach a broader audience. For instance, a financial consulting firm might excel in personal finance while also branching into business advisory services. By diversifying its offerings, the firm not only expands its market reach but also establishes itself as a multifaceted player in the financial landscape—much like the hippo, which thrives in both water and land environments.

Finding a unique market position requires continuous exploration and adaptation. Just as hippos engage in social behaviours, communicating with one another and forming groups, businesses can benefit from collaboration and networking. Engaging with industry peers, seeking partnerships, or participating in community initiatives can help enhance visibility and create opportunities for differentiation. Collaboration can yield new ideas, innovative approaches, and a stronger market presence.

In conclusion, the hippo's unique nature serves as a powerful reminder of the importance of differentiation in the financial world. By embracing your distinct strengths, crafting a compelling brand narrative, and exploring diverse avenues for growth, you can carve out your niche in the marketplace. Just as the hippo reigns supreme in both land and water, you too can establish a strong presence in the financial landscape, standing out amid the competition and thriving in your unique space.

The Strength of the Hippo: Harnessing Inner Resources

In the heart of Africa's rivers, the hippo reigns as a symbol of power and resilience. With a colossal frame and formidable jaws, these creatures command respect, establishing dominance over their territory. One striking example of their strength and unity came when a crocodile preyed upon a baby hippo, igniting a fierce response from the adult hippos. With their instinct for protection driving them, the mothers rallied the group, showcasing their power and solidarity. In a coordinated effort, the hippos charged the crocodile, using their size and strength to their advantage. Together, they turned the tide, driving the predator away and demonstrating that when united, their inner resources were unparalleled.

Yet, their strength isn't solely physical; it's also about knowing how to harness and utilize their inner resources effectively. In the world of finance, this concept resonates deeply, illustrating how individuals and businesses can tap into their own strengths to build a robust foundation for success.

Every hippo is equipped with unique abilities—whether it's their social intelligence, adaptability in aquatic environments, or sheer physical might. Similarly, each person possesses strengths that can be leveraged for financial growth. Recognizing and identifying these strengths is the first step. Are you an exceptional communicator? Do you have a knack for numbers? Perhaps your creativity sets you apart. Just as hippos utilize their physical capabilities to thrive, you must embrace your core competencies and find ways to integrate them into your financial strategies.

Leveraging these strengths means actively seeking opportunities that align with your skills. For instance, if you're adept at networking, you might explore avenues in sales or business development where relationship-building is crucial. Or, if you excel at data analysis, you might consider roles in financial planning or investment management, where your analytical skills can shine. The hippo's ability to dominate both land and water serves as a reminder that versatility is key. Just as these animals navigate different terrains with ease, you too should be willing to adapt your skills to various financial landscapes.

Establishing a strong financial position involves not just recognizing your strengths but also having the confidence to utilize them. Hippos don't shy away from their size; they embrace it, using it to protect themselves and their young. In your financial life, this translates to having the courage to make bold decisions based on your unique skill set. Whether it's starting a new venture, negotiating a raise, or investing in further education, leveraging your inner resources can propel you forward in the face of uncertainty.

Ultimately, the strength of the hippo teaches us that true power comes from within. By harnessing your inner resources and aligning them with your financial goals, you can carve out a path to success that is both sustainable and fulfilling. Embrace your strengths, navigate the waters of financial opportunity, and establish a territory where you can thrive.

The Power of Community and Strength

In the vast landscape of life, the hippo stands as a symbol of unity and resilience. When faced with the tragedy of losing a baby to a crocodile, the hippo community came together, showcasing the strength that lies in collaboration. Their unwavering resolve transformed grief into action, leading to a powerful demonstration of solidarity as they united to confront their predator. This event serves as a poignant reminder: in times of crisis, it is the bonds we forge and the communities we build that empower us to overcome even the gravest challenges.

Just as the hippos rely on their social dynamics to navigate the complexities of their environment, we too can harness the power of relationships in the financial realm. Building networks and collaborating with others can unlock doors to new opportunities, provide invaluable support, and ultimately lead to greater success. Embracing the spirit of community not only strengthens our financial positions but also enriches our lives, fostering an environment where everyone can thrive.

As we conclude this exploration of the hippo and its remarkable attributes, let us carry forward the lessons learned: the importance of recognizing our strengths, remaining adaptable in the face of adversity, identifying and managing risks, standing out through differentiation, and leveraging the power of collaboration. In the jungle of life, where challenges are inevitable, it is these principles that will guide us toward financial prosperity and resilience.

Now, as we prepare to venture into the next chapter, remember that the journey through the jungle is not just about survival; it's about thriving, embracing change, and working together to create a future where we can all flourish. Keep your eyes open for the opportunities that lie ahead, for like the hippos, we have the strength, endurance, and community spirit to navigate the currents of life and emerge victorious.

Chapter Five: Buffalo – The Relentless Defender

The buffalo stands as a symbol of resilience and brute force in the wild, embodying a mixture of sheer power and strategic survival. With its hulking frame, sturdy horns, and tough hide, the buffalo possesses the physical advantages that allow it to navigate the harsh savanna. When threatened, this massive animal doesn't flee in panic but squares up to its adversary, ready to defend itself at all costs. Its agility is deceptive, moving swiftly to outmanoeuvre predators while using its bulk to ram or trample anything in its path.

Yet, it's not just physical prowess that sets the buffalo apart it's the spirit of survival ingrained in its nature. When faced with life-threatening situations, the buffalo switches into a serious mode of self-defence, fighting fiercely for its life, even when surrounded by a pack of lions. In a stand-off, a buffalo will not retreat easily. Instead, it fights relentlessly, charging headfirst into danger. Even though the odds may be stacked against it, and there are times when it is overpowered and ends up as prey, the buffalo's tenacity never wavers. It fights until the very end, embodying the essence of never giving up in the face of overwhelming odds.

This chapter draws lessons from the buffalo's perseverance and survival instincts, exploring how we can adapt its mindset when dealing with financial adversity, knowing that strength alone isn't enough it's the refusal to back down that defines true resilience.

FACING THE PREDATOR: Standing Your Ground in Financial Battles

When a buffalo senses danger, it doesn't turn and run—at least not right away. Instead, it assesses the situation, gathers its strength, and prepares to face the predator head-on. With sheer power and resilience, the buffalo digs its hooves into the ground, snorts a warning, and braces for the inevitable clash. Even when surrounded by a pack of lions, buffaloes don't surrender easily. They stand firm, leveraging their physical strength, agility, and group dynamics to protect themselves. Sometimes they survive; other times, they succumb, but not without putting up a fight.

In the financial world, this same resolve is critical. When a market downturn hits, competition threatens to erode your business, or debt starts to loom like a predator circling its prey, standing your ground becomes a necessary strategy. The buffalo's instinct to defend itself mirrors the approach individuals and businesses should take when faced with financial battles. Rather than fleeing from financial threats, you need a well-built defence strategy that ensures your assets are protected, your risks minimized, and your long-term success secured.

Defensive financial strategies are essential when market conditions become hostile. Just as a buffalo will use its horns to fend off an attack, you need tools like **diversification** to spread risk across different investments. By not putting all your financial resources in one place, you reduce the likelihood of a single financial threat wiping out your entire portfolio. In the same way that buffaloes gather in herds for protection, collaboration with other businesses or professionals can help share the burden and defend against competitive pressures.

When a predator strikes, a buffalo has the **instinct to assess the threat** before reacting—knowing when to charge and when to conserve energy. This translates into smart financial decision-making. Before reacting to a downturn or a challenging situation, analyse the risks carefully. Implementing **risk management strategies** allows you to assess the potential financial threats, calculate their impact, and prepare accordingly. It's about maintaining a strategic position where you can stand your ground without exposing yourself to unnecessary dangers. Building an **emergency fund** or **reserve capital** is a perfect way to give yourself breathing room in case of sudden financial hits.

Just like a buffalo that stands tall, ready to defend its life even in the face of overwhelming odds, businesses and individuals must be prepared to fight off financial predators. Whether it's **protecting investments from market volatility** or creating a **solid budget to handle debt**, the key lies in resilience. Even if the financial 'predator' seems insurmountable at first glance, the determination to stand your ground anchored by a strong defence strategy will often turn the tide in your favour.

Buffaloes don't give up easily, and neither should you. In financial battles, the strongest defence is a combination of awareness, preparedness, and a refusal to be easily defeated. No matter how fierce the predator may seem, those who stand firm, protect what's theirs, and adapt to the challenge often emerge stronger on the other side.

Surviving Harsh Environments: Thriving in Adversity

In the unforgiving savanna, the buffalo has earned a reputation for its remarkable ability to endure some of the toughest environment's nature can offer. Whether it's drought season, lack of food, or relentless predators, the buffalo doesn't just survive it adapts and thrives, finding ways to move forward when the odds seem insurmountable. They push through the harshest conditions, relying on their resilience, strength, and the instinct to never give up.

For businesses and individuals facing tough financial environments, such as recessions or market downturns, the buffalo's perseverance serves as a powerful metaphor. When economic conditions take a turn for the worse, you may find yourself in a similar fight for survival. Income may slow, expenses could rise, and opportunities might dry up. However, just as the buffalo weathers droughts and evades predators, it is possible to not only survive but find ways to thrive in the face of financial adversity.

Resilience is the cornerstone of thriving through tough times. Much like how buffaloes endure extreme heat or limited food resources, you must build financial resilience by ensuring your resources can withstand periods of reduced cash flow. This could mean **bolstering your emergency fund** or creating a leaner, more efficient business model to cut down on unnecessary costs. Just as a buffalo conserves energy during droughts, being **strategic with your spending** can help you stretch your financial resources and ensure that they last through the toughest stretches.

Navigating economic downturns also requires **adaptability**. When predators or droughts threaten a buffalo's usual grazing path, it shifts direction, sometimes moving miles in search of greener pastures. Similarly, businesses and individuals facing financial crises must be willing to **pivot strategies** when necessary. This could mean shifting your business model to meet new market demands, exploring **alternative revenue streams**, or even diversifying your income sources to stay afloat. Just as buffalo herds migrate to safer areas, you may need to **explore new markets** or pivot to meet changing customer needs.

Maintaining **financial stability in challenging times** means making smart, proactive decisions. In the same way that buffaloes huddle together to protect one another from predators, you can lean on your **network of partners, investors, or advisors** to navigate tough situations. Collaboration can provide the strength needed to withstand a financial storm, and you may even find that tough times foster innovation and growth, just as scarcity pushes buffaloes to find new resources and paths for survival.

Thriving in adversity requires an unbreakable mindset. Even when the environment around you seems hostile whether it's a market crash, rising inflation, or a global financial crisis the buffalo teaches us the power of endurance. It's not about being untouched by the storm, but about **weathering the challenges**, emerging stronger, and finding opportunities where others see only obstacles.

When the dust of the economic storm settles, those who've built the resilience to adapt, conserve resources, and stand strong in the face of adversity will emerge not just as survivors, but as leaders just like the buffalo, standing firm even in the harshest environments.

Enduring Pain: Pushing Through Financial Setbacks

The buffalo, despite its immense strength and power, is no stranger to pain. Whether it's from a battle with predators or injuries sustained while navigating the harsh savanna, these animals have developed the remarkable ability to endure serious wounds and keep moving forward. You might see a buffalo bleeding, limping, and yet still charging ahead with unwavering determination. It's a survival instinct, a refusal to succumb to the harshness of life, no matter how much it hurts. This endurance mirrors the resilience needed to push through financial setbacks.

In the financial world, setbacks are inevitable. Businesses may experience sudden drops in revenue, unexpected expenses, or even catastrophic losses. On a personal level, you might face overwhelming debt, investment failures, or financial decisions that didn't turn out as expected. Just like the buffalo charging through its pain, it's essential to adopt the mindset that setbacks are not the end they are part of the journey.

Financial recovery is about more than just patching up the wounds; it's about having a clear, **long-term plan** that allows you to push through even when the immediate future looks bleak. Imagine a buffalo that's injured in a fight rather than giving up, it retreats temporarily to heal, regains its strength, and re-enters the fray stronger than before. Financially, this means taking the time to reassess, regroup, and **strategize**. Whether it's consolidating debt, cutting losses on a failed investment, or rebuilding your savings, each step is a part of the healing process.

But healing alone isn't enough you need the **perseverance to push through financial hardship**. Much like how a buffalo keeps moving forward despite injuries, you must stay committed to your financial goals even when setbacks threaten to throw you off course. This could mean rethinking your budget, cutting back on unnecessary expenses, or even seeking out new income streams to bridge the gap during difficult times. Resilience means refusing to let short-term pain derail long-term success.

Perseverance in finance often requires you to shift your perspective from short-term discomfort to long-term gain. A business that loses a key client or suffers a market dip may feel the immediate sting, but with the right mindset, those short-term losses can be transformed into opportunities. Whether it's diversifying income sources, rebranding, or adjusting your investment strategy, pushing through pain often leads to stronger, more stable financial growth in the future.

Setbacks, like a buffalo's battle scars, tell a story of endurance. They are marks of survival, not defeat. The ability to **endure financial pain** and come out the other side isn't just about surviving it's about learning, adapting, and continuing the fight with greater wisdom and resilience. You don't give up because the road gets hard; you dig in, just like the buffalo, and keep moving forward, trusting that your persistence will lead to long-term success.

In the end, those who push through financial setbacks, enduring the temporary pain, will find themselves in a stronger position than before, having learned valuable lessons, built resilience, and proven their ability to thrive no matter the circumstances. Just like the buffalo, you may walk away with scars, but you'll also walk away as a survivor.

STRENGTH IN NUMBERS: The Power of Collective Defence

When a buffalo is threatened by predators, it doesn't face the danger alone. Instead, it calls upon its herd, and together they form a formidable line of defence. These animals understand that survival isn't just about individual strength; it's about the **power of unity**. By relying on each other, they significantly increase their chances of warding off danger and surviving attacks. This instinctive behaviour in the wild demonstrates the immense advantage of strength in numbers, a lesson that is just as relevant in the financial world.

In the business and financial landscape, the idea of "going it alone" can be tempting, but it often leads to vulnerability. Much like the lone buffalo becomes easy prey, businesses and individuals that operate in isolation during tough financial times can find themselves exposed to risks they may not be able to fend off alone. This is where the **power of networking, collaboration, and partnerships** comes into play.

During financial challenges whether it's a market downturn, increased competition, or even an unexpected crisis having a strong network or community to rely on can make all the difference. **Networking** allows you to tap into resources and knowledge that you wouldn't have access to on your own. Just as a buffalo turns to its herd for protection, individuals and businesses can turn to their networks for **advice, mentorship, and opportunities**. This could mean seeking the counsel of financial advisors, leveraging the experiences of peers in your industry, or collaborating with others to share risks and find solutions.

Collaboration also plays a key role in ensuring financial security. Businesses can form **strategic partnerships** to pool resources, share expertise, and create a collective buffer against economic downturns. For example, during a recession, companies that collaborate on joint ventures or share operational costs are more likely to survive than those that try to weather the storm alone. Much like a herd of buffalo standing shoulder to shoulder, the strength of your business alliances can provide mutual protection, allowing everyone involved to face challenges with greater resilience.

On an individual level, the same concept applies. Building strong **community support** whether through professional associations, peer groups, or even personal networks offers a safety net during difficult financial times. Just as a buffalo's survival depends on the collective defence of the herd, individuals benefit from having a trusted circle they can rely on. This support can come in the form of emotional encouragement, shared resources, or practical advice on navigating financial difficulties. The power of community should never be underestimated.

Moreover, the herd mentality in buffaloes teaches us the importance of **leveraging partnerships for financial protection**. In times of uncertainty, partnering with like-minded individuals or organizations can reduce risk, enhance stability, and open new avenues for growth. Whether it's through joint investments, shared financial ventures, or simply pooling resources to withstand economic pressure, partnerships can provide a protective shield, much like the herd protects its members from predators.

In essence, financial strength isn't just about individual prowess; it's about recognizing when to unite with others. The **power of collective defence** whether through networking, collaboration, or community support can provide a solid foundation during even the most challenging times. Just as buffaloes stand stronger together, businesses and individuals can thrive when they leverage the strength of their networks. It's not just about surviving financial challenges it's about emerging from them stronger, supported, and ready to face the next wave of opportunities.

THE PERILS OF OVERCONFIDENCE: When Strength Becomes a Weakness

Buffaloes, with their immense size and collective strength, are formidable creatures, often able to stand their ground against some of the fiercest predators. Yet, their power can sometimes lead to overconfidence. There are moments when a buffalo, emboldened by its own might, ventures too far from the safety of the herd or engages in a battle it cannot win. When faced with multiple predators, that same strength becomes a liability, as overconfidence blinds it to the danger. In these moments, the buffalo can find itself overwhelmed, trapped by its own misplaced belief in invincibility.

This dynamic plays out in the financial world as well. **Overconfidence**, while it can be empowering, can also lead to poor decisions. When individuals or businesses feel untouchable after a string of financial successes, for instance they may take unnecessary risks, ignore potential threats, or become reckless with their investments. Just as a buffalo stray from the herd thinking it can handle a predator alone; financial overconfidence often leads people to **overestimate their ability** to navigate complex or volatile markets.

Reckless investments are one of the most common ways this overconfidence manifests. It's easy to feel invincible when the markets are booming or when you've had several wins in a row. But that same confidence can drive individuals to **place high-stakes bets** on risky ventures or invest without proper research or risk management. Much like the buffalo that doesn't recognize the lurking danger of multiple predators, these investors may not see the financial traps awaiting them whether it's an overheated market, an unsustainable trend, or a too-good-to-be-true opportunity.

Taking on too much risk is another symptom of financial overconfidence. Buffalos that charge headlong into danger, believing their strength will carry them through, often find themselves caught in situations they can't control. Similarly, when people take on excessive financial risk by overleveraging, borrowing too much, or placing too much capital in a single investment they expose themselves to **massive losses** that can be difficult to recover from. Overconfidence, in these cases, leads to a false sense of security, blinding them to the potential consequences if the tide turns.

Ignoring potential threats is another dangerous byproduct of overconfidence. In the wild, a buffalo may be so focused on one predator that it misses the others stalking in the shadows. In financial terms, this occurs when businesses or individuals **fail to diversify their investments** or **overlook red flags** in the market. Overconfidence makes them blind to vulnerabilities in their portfolio, competitive threats, or changes in market dynamics that could jeopardize their financial position.

The lesson here is not to avoid confidence, but to **balance it with caution**. Confidence is necessary for financial success, but when it tips into arrogance, it becomes a weakness. Like the buffalo, whose sheer power can sometimes lead it into danger, individuals and businesses must recognize when their strength could work against them.

Staying vigilant and humble is key. **Risk assessment** should always be part of the equation, even when things are going well. Just as a buffalo must constantly scan its environment for predators, businesses and individuals need to **remain aware of market trends**, potential risks, and the broader economic landscape. Confidence should never lead to complacency.

In the end, strength whether in the wild or financial matters is only truly valuable when it's paired with **wisdom and humility**. The **perils of overconfidence** serve as a reminder that no matter how successful or powerful you may feel, there are always risks lurking. By staying grounded, making well-considered decisions, and avoiding the temptation of reckless financial choices, you can ensure that your strength remains an asset, rather than a liability.

The Resilience of the Buffalo

As we step back from the rugged terrain where the buffalo roams, it's clear that these majestic creatures embody the essence of resilience and tenacity. They face a world filled with predators, harsh environments, and countless challenges, yet they thrive through sheer determination and unity. In the financial realm, we can learn much from the buffalo's journey.

The buffalo teaches us the importance of **standing our ground** when financial threats arise. Just as they face off against predators, we must confront market downturns, fierce competition, and the lurking shadows of debt. Developing a **solid defence strategy** is paramount; this means protecting our investments and crafting a robust financial plan that can weather the storms of uncertainty.

Moreover, buffaloes thrive in adversity, proving that even in the most challenging economic climates, resilience can be a powerful ally. They remind us that, like them, we can endure harsh conditions whether they be recessions or personal financial crises. This journey is about maintaining **financial stability**, even when the odds seem stacked against us.

Buffaloes endure pain, whether from battles with rivals or injuries sustained during confrontations. In the same way, setbacks in our financial journey are inevitable. However, embracing a mindset of perseverance will pave the way for recovery and success.

The scars we bear can serve as lessons learned, fuelling our long-term planning and determination to push through.

Unity is another invaluable lesson from the buffalo's herd. Strength in numbers be it through networking, collaboration, or community support can be a vital component of financial protection. In times of crisis, leaning on our networks can provide the security and resources needed to navigate turbulent waters.

Yet, we must also heed the warning of overconfidence. Just as the buffalo's pride can lead it into precarious situations, we too must remain vigilant. Financial success does not come from reckless decisions or ignoring potential risks; it stems from a balanced approach that combines confidence with caution.

In the end, the buffalo stands as a symbol of what it means to be strong, adaptable, and community oriented. By embracing these qualities, we can navigate the financial landscape with the same grace and grit as these incredible creatures. The journey ahead may be fraught with challenges, but like the buffalo, we must harness our inner strength and face the future with unwavering resolve.

Chapter Six: Meerkats – The Guardians of the Colony

In the vast, sun-soaked expanses of the African savanna, a remarkable community of creatures exemplifies the power of teamwork and vigilance: the meerkats. Standing no taller than a loaf of bread, these small mammals embody a remarkable blend of agility and intelligence. With their sharp eyes scanning the horizon and their ears perked for the slightest rustle, meerkats are nature's sentinels, alert to potential dangers that threaten their close-knit family group.

As the sun rises over the savanna, the colony emerges from their underground burrows, ready to face the day. But what sets meerkats apart is not just their watchful eyes or their swift movements; it's their unparalleled sense of cooperation. While one or two stand guard, the rest venture out in search of food, foraging for insects and small plants. This intricate dance of duty allows them to thrive in a world filled with predators—each member plays a crucial role, in ensuring the survival of the whole.

In the financial realm, just as in the meerkat colony, success is often a result of collective effort and a proactive mindset. Individuals and businesses that adopt a vigilant approach to their finances, stay informed, and work together can better navigate the unpredictable currents of the economic landscape. As we delve into the world of meerkats, we'll uncover valuable insights about community, adaptability, and resilience—lessons that can empower us to become guardians of our financial futures.

The Power of Collective Intelligence: Wisdom in Numbers

In the bustling underground world of meerkats, every member plays a pivotal role in the colony's survival. With their keen senses and unique abilities, they form a tightly knit community that thrives on cooperation. When one meerkat stands watch for predators, others forage for food or care for the young, creating a synergy that ensures the group's safety and sustenance. This collaboration extends beyond mere protection; it is a finely tuned system of information sharing. Each meerkat brings insights from their individual experiences, creating a tapestry of knowledge that bolsters the entire colony's chances of thriving in a harsh environment.

In the financial realm, this idea of collective intelligence resonates deeply. Just as meerkats rely on one another to navigate dangers, individuals and businesses can benefit immensely from the collective insights of their networks. Collaboration can lead to more informed decision-making, as sharing knowledge and perspectives from diverse backgrounds allows for a broader understanding of the landscape. When making investment choices or strategic business moves, tapping into a collective intelligence pool can illuminate opportunities and risks that might otherwise go unnoticed.

For instance, a small business owner may find themselves at a crossroads, unsure whether to invest in new technology or expand their product line. By engaging with a network of fellow entrepreneurs, they can gather opinions based on a range of experiences. One peer might share insights from a similar investment that yielded unexpected returns, while another might caution against overspending in uncertain economic times. This wealth of knowledge not only aids in making a more informed decision but also fosters innovation. Collaborative brainstorming sessions can lead to fresh ideas, allowing businesses to pivot and adapt in ways that a solitary approach might miss.

Moreover, the digital age has created unparalleled opportunities for collaboration. Online forums, social media, and professional networks enable individuals to connect, share insights, and learn from one another regardless of geographical barriers. This democratization of information means that anyone can tap into the collective wisdom of others, leveraging diverse perspectives to enhance their financial strategies.

Embracing the concept of collective intelligence can also foster a culture of accountability and support. When individuals collaborate and share their successes and failures, they create an environment where learning becomes a shared journey. Just as meerkats look out for one another, so too can financial communities empower each member to thrive, ensuring that knowledge is not hoarded but instead freely exchanged.

Ultimately, the strength of collective intelligence lies in its ability to transform decision-making processes. By prioritizing collaboration and knowledge-sharing, individuals and businesses can navigate the complexities of the financial landscape with greater confidence. As meerkats demonstrate, survival is not solely about individual prowess; it's about leveraging the wisdom and experiences of the entire community.

STAY ALERT: THE IMPORTANCE of Proactive Monitoring

In the sun-drenched plains of the savanna, the meerkat colony thrives, not just because of their social bonds but due to their unyielding vigilance. With their sharp eyes scanning the horizon and their ears perked for the slightest rustle, these tiny sentinels embody the essence of being alert. When one meerkat stands sentinel, a sense of safety blankets the entire group; they are ready to respond at a moment's notice, ensuring their collective survival. This proactive monitoring is not merely a habit; it's a way of life, ingrained in their very existence.

Translating this principle to the financial world reveals a critical lesson: proactive monitoring is essential for maintaining financial health and resilience. Just as meerkats keep a watchful eye on potential threats, individuals and businesses must regularly assess their financial conditions to identify potential dangers before they escalate. In the rapidly changing landscape of today's economy, staying informed about market fluctuations, investment performance, and emerging risks can mean the difference between success and failure.

For individuals, proactive monitoring begins with a regular review of personal finances. Setting a schedule—be it monthly or quarterly—to assess your budget, savings, and expenses ensures that you're not only aware of where your money is going but also able to identify areas that need adjustment. This practice allows for a clearer understanding of financial health, revealing potential issues such as overspending or inadequate savings well before they become crises.

Businesses, too, must prioritize proactive monitoring. Regularly reviewing financial statements, tracking key performance indicators (KPIs), and conducting market analyses can unveil trends that may signal potential downturns or opportunities for growth. For instance, a business experiencing stagnation in sales may benefit from investigating changing consumer preferences or economic shifts. By staying ahead of the curve, businesses can pivot their strategies to adapt to new realities, much like a meerkat quickly alters its behavior in response to an imminent threat.

Additionally, leveraging technology can significantly enhance proactive monitoring efforts. Financial apps and software can provide real-time insights into spending habits, investment performance, and market trends. Setting alerts for significant changes in stock prices or market conditions can empower individuals and businesses to act quickly when necessary. This level of engagement fosters a mindset of vigilance, creating an awareness that enables informed decisions rather than reactive measures.

Moreover, cultivating a habit of continuous learning can further enhance awareness of potential threats. Engaging with financial news, attending workshops, or participating in online courses keeps individuals informed about economic shifts, investment strategies, and risk management techniques. Just as meerkats learn from each other's experiences, sharing knowledge within networks can bolster collective vigilance and preparedness.

Ultimately, staying alert in the financial realm is about creating a culture of awareness and proactivity. By implementing regular monitoring practices, leveraging technology, and fostering a commitment to ongoing learning, individuals and businesses can navigate the complexities of the financial landscape with confidence. Much like the meerkats who protect their colony through constant vigilance, maintaining a proactive approach to financial monitoring ensures readiness to tackle challenges before they arise, securing a path toward sustained success.

Adaptation as a Strategy: Flexibility in Financial Planning

In the sprawling desert, the meerkat family exemplifies resilience through adaptation. When food becomes scarce, these resourceful creatures don't simply resign to hunger; they modify their foraging strategies, shifting their focus to what is available. Whether it's hunting for insects under rocks or scouring the area for succulent roots, meerkats demonstrate that flexibility can be a matter of survival. This lesson in adaptability extends beyond the wild and into the realm of financial planning, where the ability to adjust to changing circumstances can significantly influence long-term success.

In the dynamic world of finance, the only constant is change. Economic conditions can shift rapidly, and what works today may not be effective tomorrow. Individuals and businesses that rigidly adhere to outdated financial plans risk stagnation or, worse, failure. Embracing flexibility in financial planning empowers them to navigate the uncertainties of the market effectively.

First and foremost, a key aspect of flexible financial planning is the willingness to revise budgets regularly. Life can throw unexpected expenses our way—be it medical bills, home repairs, or fluctuations in income. Just as meerkats change their foraging habits based on food availability, individuals must be prepared to reassess their budgets considering new realities. This means allocating funds to priority areas, trimming unnecessary expenditures, and ensuring that savings goals remain attainable despite shifting circumstances.

Additionally, exploring new investment avenues is crucial in a world where opportunities can emerge unexpectedly. The most successful investors are those who keep an eye on market trends and are willing to pivot their strategies when necessary. For instance, if a particular sector shows signs of decline, a flexible investor might diversify their portfolio by exploring emerging markets or industries. The key is to remain open to change, leveraging research and analysis to make informed decisions. Just as meerkats share knowledge about the best foraging spots, engaging with financial advisors or investment communities can provide valuable insights into new opportunities.

Moreover, adaptability also encompasses responding to economic conditions. During times of economic downturn, it's vital to reassess investment strategies and risk tolerance. A meerkat wouldn't continue to forage in a barren area; instead, it would seek out more fruitful grounds. Similarly, individuals may need to adjust their investment portfolios to minimize risk during volatile periods, shifting towards safer assets or more stable sectors. This proactive approach can safeguard against significant losses while allowing for growth when conditions improve.

Flexibility is not just about reacting to change but also about anticipating it. Individuals and businesses should cultivate a mindset that embraces innovation and evolution. This means being proactive about learning new financial strategies, exploring different income streams, and seeking knowledge about emerging market trends. Just as meerkats continuously adapt to their environment, maintaining a willingness to learn can open doors to new possibilities and ensure that financial plans remain relevant and effective.

In conclusion, the meerkat's survival hinges on its ability to adapt, and the same principle applies to financial planning. By embracing flexibility in budgeting, exploring new investment avenues, and responding proactively to changing economic conditions, individuals and businesses can navigate the unpredictable landscape of finance. The ability to adapt becomes not just a survival tactic but a strategic advantage that fosters long-term financial success. Like the meerkat colony thriving against the odds, those who cultivate adaptability in their financial strategies will find themselves better equipped to flourish, no matter the challenges they face.

Leadership Beyond Authority: Fostering a Culture of Trust

In the intricate social structure of a meerkat colony, leadership is not confined to a single dominant figure; rather, it is a dynamic tapestry woven from the strengths and contributions of each member. At different times, various meerkats take the lead, whether it's foraging for food, keeping watch for predators, or teaching young ones the ropes. This shared approach to leadership fosters a culture of trust and collaboration, proving that effective guidance is rooted not in authority but in empowerment and mutual respect.

In the realm of finance, a similar ethos can transform how teams operate, and projects unfold. Trust-based leadership encourages open communication, where team members feel safe to share their insights and ideas. This culture of openness can significantly enhance financial projects, leading to more innovative solutions and robust strategies. When individuals believe their contributions are valued, they are more likely to invest effort and creativity into their work, much like how a meerkat bravely takes on the responsibility of sentinel to safeguard the colony.

Empowering teams is at the heart of this leadership approach. Instead of a top-down directive style, fostering a sense of ownership among team members encourages them to take initiative and be proactive. For example, in financial planning or investment strategy discussions, allowing each team member to express their opinions can lead to richer, more well-rounded decision-making. Just as meerkats rely on the diverse skills and experiences of their colony members, organizations benefit from a variety of perspectives. This collaborative environment not only strengthens the final outcomes but also nurtures individual growth, as team members learn from one another and refine their skills.

Moreover, shared leadership can play a critical role during times of uncertainty or financial challenges. When the going gets tough, it's essential to rely on the collective intelligence of the group. A meerkat group excels at quickly reallocating roles based on the situation—one might step up as a lookout while another leads the foraging. Similarly, financial teams can thrive in adversity by distributing responsibilities according to strengths, allowing for a more agile response to challenges. This fluidity builds resilience, as everyone feels invested in the process and outcome, bolstering the overall morale of the group.

To cultivate this culture of trust and collaboration, organizations can implement several strategies. Regularly scheduled meetings that promote dialogue and feedback can help ensure everyone feels heard. Establishing mentorship programs can also encourage knowledge sharing and build relationships within the team. Additionally, recognizing and celebrating team achievements fosters a sense of belonging and reinforces the value of collaborative efforts. Just as meerkats groom each other to strengthen their bonds, organizations that prioritize interpersonal connections create a more supportive and effective work environment.

Finally, it's essential to remember that trust in leadership must be reciprocal. Leaders should not only empower their teams but also be transparent in their decision-making processes and admit when they need help. This vulnerability can inspire team members to be more open, creating a cycle of trust and collaboration that echoes through the organization. When leaders actively engage with their teams and encourage shared responsibility, they set the stage for a thriving financial culture that drives success. The meerkat's shared leadership model teaches us invaluable lessons about fostering a culture of trust within organizations. By encouraging input, empowering teams, and embracing collaborative decision-making, financial leaders can enhance project outcomes and cultivate a positive environment. As we navigate the complexities of the financial world, let us take a page from the meerkat playbook, recognizing that true leadership lies in uplifting others and creating a community where everyone thrives together.

EMBRACING THE MEERKAT Way in Financial Leadership

In the grand theatre of life, where the smallest creatures often showcase the most profound lessons, the meerkat stands as a shining example of collaboration and trust. As David Attenborough once illustrated in his captivating narratives, the interconnectedness of nature is a testament to the power of unity, where every member of a community plays a vital role in the survival and success of the whole. Just as meerkats thrive through their collective intelligence and shared leadership, so too can we embrace these principles within the financial realm.

In today's dynamic and often tumultuous financial landscape, the call for adaptive leadership has never been more critical. It's not merely about having the loudest voice in the room; it's about nurturing an environment where diverse perspectives are not just welcomed but actively sought out. By fostering trust and collaboration, organizations can weather the storms of uncertainty and emerge stronger, much like a meerkat colony that stands vigilant against the predators lurking nearby.

Moreover, the lessons gleaned from the meerkat's intricate social structure serve as a reminder of the importance of agility and resilience. In times of economic turmoil, organizations must pivot and adapt, relying on the shared wisdom of their teams. This collaborative spirit not only enhances decision-making but also cultivates a culture where every individual feels valued and empowered, driving innovation and success.

As we reflect on the nature of financial leadership, let us take inspiration from the meerkat's way of life. In a world that often prizes individualism, we can forge paths of collective strength, ensuring that no one is left behind. Let us embrace the notion that true leadership flourishes in the soil of trust and cooperation, where every member of the team contributes to the greater good.

In this dance of financial survival and growth, we must remember that, like the meerkats of the savanna, we are stronger together. Let us stride forward with the knowledge that by embracing shared leadership and nurturing our community, we can not only face the challenges ahead but thrive in the face of adversity, securing our place in the intricate tapestry of the financial world.

Chapter Seven: Hyenas – The Opportunistic Survivors

In the vast African savannah, the high-pitched laughter of hyenas echoes across the plains. Though often misunderstood as mere scavengers, hyenas are some of the most skilled and strategic predators, known for their resourcefulness and survival instincts. They adapt quickly, work in packs, and seize every opportunity, turning unfavourable situations into advantages. Whether they're outsmarting lions or capitalizing on the leftovers of other predators, hyenas embody the art of thriving through cunning and calculated risk-taking.

In the financial world, we can learn much from these remarkable animals. They teach us the value of flexibility, seizing opportunities when others overlook them, and staying relentless in the pursuit of success, even in the face of adversity. Like hyenas who band together for a coordinated attack, individuals and businesses must be strategic, resourceful, and willing to collaborate to navigate complex financial environments. This chapter dives into how we can harness the principles of survival, adaptability, and resourcefulness from the hyena to achieve financial success.

As we explore the cunning nature of the hyena, we'll uncover lessons on spotting hidden opportunities, taking calculated risks, and the importance of working together to fend off challenges. Just as hyenas thrive in an unpredictable world, this chapter will show

how we, too, can rise above financial challenges by tapping into our inner opportunist, remaining adaptable, and refusing to give up.

FLEXIBILITY IN THE Face of Adversity: Adapting to Changing Markets

In the heart of the savanna, hyenas are the masters of adaptability. Whether the lion's share of the hunt has already been claimed, or the herds have moved on, hyenas find a way to thrive. Sometimes they scavenge; sometimes they hunt in packs, adjusting their methods to whatever the situation demands. This resilience in the face of uncertainty is what sets them apart, ensuring survival even in the harshest conditions. Their strength lies not in brute force but in their ability to read the environment and change their tactics as necessary.

The financial world is no different. Economic landscapes shift without warning—one moment, you're riding a bull market, and the next, you're staring down a recession. Much like the hyena adapts its hunting strategy, individuals and businesses must remain agile in the face of financial adversity. The ability to pivot when the market changes, reassess investment strategies, or find new income streams is key to not just surviving but thriving in volatile conditions.

A flexible financial strategy means understanding that what worked yesterday might not work tomorrow. It's about having the foresight to diversify investments, explore new opportunities, and, like the hyena, capitalize on every available resource. Just as a hyena will switch from hunting to scavenging when necessary, savvy investors may need to shift focus—whether that's pulling out of risky assets, exploring more conservative options, or seeking alternative markets.

This flexibility is not just a defensive strategy; it's an offensive one. By anticipating challenges and being prepared to pivot, you can not only withstand financial adversity but also find new opportunities in the chaos. Markets that appear desolate at first glance may still hold opportunities for those willing to adapt. The key is to stay alert, remain agile, and be ready to shift your approach when the financial climate demands it.

In uncertain times, being rigid in your financial strategy is a risk, but being adaptable like the hyena can make all the difference between failure and long-term success. The goal is not to fight the changing tides but to flow with them, adjusting strategies and moving forward stronger than before.

Seizing the Moment: Capitalizing on Financial Opportunities

In the wild, hyenas are the embodiment of opportunism. They don't wait for the perfect conditions; they act swiftly when a chance presents itself—whether it's an injured animal, abandoned prey, or even leftovers from another predator. To a hyena, every opportunity is a potential meal, and they've learned to thrive by recognizing these fleeting moments that others might miss.

In the financial world, seizing the moment is equally vital. Opportunities often appear disguised as challenges or in moments of uncertainty, and those who are quick to act are the ones who profit. Just like hyenas pounce at the right time, investors and businesses must be prepared to identify undervalued assets, emerging market trends, or unconventional opportunities. Success rarely comes from waiting for the ideal set of conditions; instead, it comes from having the foresight to recognize hidden value and the courage to make bold decisions when others hesitate.

Whether it's capitalizing on a dip in the stock market, spotting a startup with potential before it takes off, or even exploring alternative investments like real estate during economic downturns, the key lies in being proactive. Hyenas don't overanalyse the situation—they assess the risk quickly, act, and adapt as needed. Similarly, in the financial world, overthinking can result in missed opportunities. Quick decision-making, backed by solid research and a keen eye for value, is essential to staying ahead.

Timing is everything. In volatile markets, opportunities can be brief, and waiting too long might mean missing out. However, being opportunistic doesn't mean being reckless—it means understanding when the odds are in your favour and acting with precision. For example, during a recession, when most are pulling out of investments in fear, those who recognize the long-term potential of undervalued stocks can make gains others overlook.

The ability to recognize and seize financial opportunities can transform small investments into significant returns and challenges into growth avenues. Hyenas don't just wait for opportunities—they create them by staying alert, acting swiftly, and understanding that in every scarcity, there is potential. The lesson here is clear: by being opportunistic, thinking strategically, and moving decisively, you can turn unexpected chances into lasting success.

RELENTLESS PURSUIT: Staying Determined in Financial Growth

Hyenas are known for their unwavering persistence. Whether hunting solo or as part of a pack, they pursue their prey with relentless focus, often traveling long distances or outlasting their target through sheer determination. Their success doesn't come from brute strength alone but from their ability to stay the course, even when the odds seem stacked against them. This relentless pursuit mirrors the path to financial growth.

In the world of finance, building wealth is rarely a quick process. It requires patience, long-term strategies, and the ability to stay committed despite obstacles. Just as hyenas don't give up after one failed chase, successful investors don't abandon their goals when the market dips or when their first investments don't yield immediate results. They know that growth takes time, and persistence is key.

A long-term investment strategy, such as buying and holding stocks, is much like the hyena's steady pursuit. It may take years to see significant returns, but those who stay committed to their financial plans, despite market fluctuations or economic downturns, are often rewarded with steady and substantial growth. This approach is particularly important during times of adversity, when fear and impatience can lead others to abandon their investments prematurely.

Moreover, just like hyenas work together to take down larger prey, collaboration in financial growth can be highly effective. Investors can benefit from pooling resources, seeking advice from mentors, or joining forces with others in a partnership. This collective effort often results in more significant gains, much like the coordinated efforts of a hyena pack.

It's also crucial to understand that setbacks are a part of the process. Hyenas don't always succeed on the first try, but they persist, adapting their approach and learning from each experience. Similarly, financial growth requires the ability to weather setbacks, learn from mistakes, and continuously improve strategies. Staying determined in the face of challenges—whether it's market volatility, economic uncertainty, or personal financial difficulties—builds resilience.

The relentless pursuit of financial success means understanding that wealth-building is a journey, not a sprint. It requires persistence, adaptability, and the determination to keep going, even when the path ahead seems tough. Like the hyena that never stops chasing its goal, successful investors and businesses thrive by staying focused on the long game, adjusting as needed, and maintaining the drive to achieve their financial goals over time.

THE ART OF PLAYING the Fool: Leveraging Underestimation for Success

Hyenas have long been cast as scavengers in the animal kingdom, often seen as lesser creatures compared to lions or leopards. Yet, beneath this misleading image lies an apex predator—highly intelligent, organized, and successful in securing its survival. What appears to be a disadvantage becomes one of their greatest strengths. They leverage their underestimated position to surprise their prey and competitors alike with strategic, well-timed actions. The same principle applies in the financial world.

In finance, perception is everything. Being underestimated or overlooked can be a powerful advantage. Investors, entrepreneurs, or businesses that operate quietly, avoid the spotlight, and focus on long-term goals often find themselves in a position of strength when their competition least expects it. Just like the hyena patiently biding its time before launching a successful hunt, those who are perceived as "small players" can seize opportunities when rivals are distracted by flashier competitors.

Take Warren Buffett, for example. Known for his modest lifestyle and unassuming demeanour, he built a reputation for not following the crowd. While many chased trends or indulged in short-term gains, Buffett quietly focused on sound, undervalued investments. His strategy of staying under the radar and avoiding the frenzy of Wall Street paid off, making him one of the wealthiest and most respected investors in history. His success, like that of the hyena, lies in surprising others with well-timed, intelligent decisions, while avoiding the pitfalls of overconfidence and flashiness.

Playing the fool doesn't mean being foolish. It's about understanding that not all success requires grandeur or attention. Sometimes, it's the quiet strategist who prevails—the one who observes, listens, and makes moves when the time is right. While competitors may be too focused on outshining each other, the savvy investor or businessperson can slip in, make strategic decisions, and capitalize on undervalued opportunities.

Being underestimated also provides an element of surprise. In negotiations, business dealings, or even market competition, those who are perceived as less of a threat often have the advantage of catching others off-guard. They can take calculated risks, move strategically, and achieve success with far less resistance. It's the same tactic hyenas use when hunting—they strike when their prey least expects it, using their intelligence to outmanoeuvre what might otherwise be a more physically dominant opponent.

In financial terms, leveraging this "art of playing the fool" means focusing on substance over style. It's about valuing long-term growth over short-term wins, quietly building your financial position, and avoiding unnecessary risks. By staying focused, avoiding flashy behaviour, and keeping a low profile, you can create opportunities that others, too caught up in the noise, will miss.

Ultimately, the art of leveraging underestimation is about turning perceived weaknesses into strengths, just as the hyena turns its reputation as a scavenger into an advantage. In the financial world, staying humble, patient, and strategically quiet can often lead to the most significant and unexpected victories.

CUNNING AND CALCULATED Risks: Thriving Through Smart Financial Manoeuvres

In the heart of the African savanna, the hyena stands out not only for its formidable strength but also for its keen intelligence and cunning. Often dismissed as mere scavengers, hyenas possess a remarkable ability to strategize and outthink their competitors. Their cleverness enables them to thrive in environments filled with challenges and uncertainties, a trait that can offer valuable lessons for financial decision-making.

Consider a hyena observing a pride of lions feasting on a recent kill. While many would view the lions as the apex predators, the hyena knows that patience and strategy can yield greater rewards. Rather than rushing in to compete directly, it waits for the opportune moment—perhaps when the lions are distracted or when a rival predator grows weary. This calculated approach allows the hyena to seize an opportunity that others may have overlooked, showcasing the importance of assessing risks intelligently.

In the financial realm, similar principles apply. Investors and entrepreneurs often face the dilemma of risk versus reward. The key lies in understanding that not all risks are created equal. Just as hyenas evaluate their environment before making a move, individuals must assess the landscape of their financial choices. This involves weighing potential gains against possible losses, considering market conditions, and recognizing when to act or hold back.

For instance, a savvy investor may identify a start-up company that shows promise but is currently undervalued. Instead of following the crowd into established, well-known stocks, they take a calculated risk by investing in the start-up, understanding both the potential for high returns and the inherent dangers of investing in a less stable entity. Much like the hyena that knows when to strike, the investor's success hinges on careful analysis and strategic timing.

Calculated risk-taking is about balance. Just as a hyena knows when to pursue its prey and when to retreat, individuals must develop the ability to read their financial situations accurately. This means cultivating a mindset that embraces both caution and courage—acknowledging that every investment carries risk while also recognizing that without taking risks, opportunities for growth may be lost.

Hyenas are also adept at working in packs, demonstrating that collaboration can enhance their chances of success. In finance, forming partnerships or alliances can similarly amplify one's ability to make smart financial moves. By pooling knowledge, resources, and perspectives, individuals can make better-informed decisions, ultimately increasing their chances of thriving in competitive environments.

The art of cunning and calculated risks is a vital component of financial success. It encourages individuals to remain vigilant, adaptable, and strategic in their approaches. By learning from the hyena's playbook—evaluating situations carefully, taking calculated chances, and embracing the strength of collaboration—individuals can position themselves to thrive even in the most challenging financial landscapes.

Let us remember that just like the cunning hyena, the path to financial success is often paved with shrewd decisions and smart manoeuvres. By cultivating a mindset of intelligence, patience, and strategy, individuals can navigate the complexities of the financial world, ensuring that they not only survive but flourish amidst competition and uncertainty.

Embracing the Hyena's Wisdom

As we draw our exploration of the hyena to a close, it becomes abundantly clear that the lessons this remarkable creature offers extend far beyond the savanna. The hyena's ability to adapt, seize opportunities, and navigate the complexities of its environment serves as a powerful metaphor for our own financial journeys. In a world rife with uncertainties and challenges, we must embody the traits of cunning and calculated risk-taking that define the hyena.

The financial landscape is ever shifting, and like the hyena, we must remain vigilant and adaptable, ready to pivot our strategies in response to market fluctuations and emerging trends. The ability to recognize opportunities, even when they are hidden in plain sight, can set us apart from the crowd. By cultivating a mindset that embraces intelligence and strategic thinking, we can position ourselves to thrive in the face of adversity.

Moreover, the hyena teaches us the value of collaboration. Just as these social animals work together to achieve their goals, we too can leverage the power of networks and partnerships. In the financial realm, fostering relationships and sharing insights can lead to greater success and innovation. It is through collaboration that we can combine our strengths, mitigate risks, and navigate the unpredictable waters of investment and entrepreneurship.

Ultimately, the journey toward financial success is not merely about avoiding risks but about understanding and managing them. The hyena's cunning nature reminds us that calculated risks can yield substantial rewards. Embrace the spirit of the hyena be vigilant, be strategic, and never underestimate the power of resilience and adaptability.

As we venture forward, let us carry these lessons with us, approaching our financial endeavours with the same tenacity and intelligence that the hyena exemplifies. In doing so, we not only honour the wisdom of this incredible creature but also empower ourselves to achieve greatness in our financial pursuits. Remember, in the wild world of finance, it is often those who dare to be cunning, calculated, and collaborative who ultimately prevail.

Chapter 8: Wild Dogs – The Masters of Collective Strategy

In the heart of the African savannah, one pack moves with an elegance few can match—the wild dogs. With unmatched coordination and communication, these canines are a symbol of unity, teamwork, and precision. They are relentless hunters, relying on their bond and trust in one another to secure survival in one of the harshest environments on earth. Each member of the pack plays a critical role, contributing to the whole in ways that allow them to outperform even the fiercest of predators.

But their strength doesn't just lie in numbers—it's in their strategy, their adaptability, and their ability to persevere. Much like the wild dogs of the savannah, individuals and businesses that operate in a fiercely competitive financial environment must learn to rely on effective collaboration, master calculated decision-making, and embrace their roles within a larger strategy. Even when faced with challenges and predators—whether they come in the form of competition or market shifts—success is forged by those who work together as a seamless unit.

David Attenborough once said, "Wild dogs live in a world of cooperation and trust, where their survival depends on the pack functioning as a single entity." And just as these animals know when to attack and when to retreat, so too must we navigate the financial jungle, with teamwork and precision guiding our way to prosperity.

In this chapter, we'll explore the key lessons wild dogs can teach us about collaboration, resilience, and the power of unity in achieving financial success. Together, we'll uncover the strategies that enable these extraordinary creatures to thrive—and how their example can inspire us to lead with strength and intelligence in the world of finance.

Chapter Eight: Wild Dogs – The Masters of Collective Strategy

In the wild, wild dogs are renowned for their extraordinary ability to work together, creating a symphony of coordination and strategy that enhances their chances of survival. Their hunting techniques are a masterclass in collaboration, showcasing how teamwork can turn the tide in even the most daunting circumstances. When a pack sets out on a hunt, each member plays a distinct role, from the skilled trackers to the relentless chasers. This unity and precision not only maximize their success in capturing prey but also embody the essence of collective effort.

This chapter will delve into the invaluable lessons that the wild dog's way of life offers, highlighting how strategic collaboration can lead to financial triumph. Whether you're a business leader forging partnership, an investor pooling resources, or an individual working towards a common goal, the principles of teamwork and shared vision are fundamental in navigating the complexities of the financial landscape.

As we explore the nuances of financial collaboration, we'll uncover how the spirit of the wild dog can inspire innovative strategies and foster a culture of unity, ultimately driving us toward our shared aspirations. The pack mentality, built on trust and mutual support, serves as a powerful metaphor for achieving success in our own financial journeys.

STRATEGIC COLLABORATION: The Blueprint for Financial Success

In the intricate dance of survival, wild dogs epitomize the power of collaboration. Their highly coordinated pack hunting strategies are not merely instinctive; they are meticulously crafted plans that hinge on trust, communication, and shared objectives. When one thinks of these remarkable creatures, it's clear that their success in the wild is a testament to the strength found in unity—a principle that holds profound implications for the world of finance and business.

In the financial realm, strategic collaboration can be the cornerstone of achieving remarkable results. Just as wild dogs leverage each member's strengths to bring down prey larger than themselves, businesses can enhance their performance by forming strategic alliances and joint ventures. These partnerships enable organizations to combine resources, share risks, and access new markets, amplifying their reach and influence.

Consider the example of investment teams, where individuals with diverse skill sets come together to make informed decisions. Each member might focus on different sectors—some on equities, others on fixed income or emerging markets—allowing the team to develop a holistic view of investment opportunities. This coordinated financial planning not only leads to more robust strategies but also fosters an environment where innovation can flourish.

However, successful collaboration requires a clear strategy. Just as wild dogs communicate effectively during a hunt to ensure that each member knows their role, businesses must establish clear goals and processes. This clarity minimizes misunderstandings and maximizes efficiency, ensuring that every participant is aligned toward a common financial objective.

Ultimately, the lessons from wild dogs remind us that strategic collaboration is not merely advantageous; it is essential for thriving in today's competitive landscape. By embracing the spirit of teamwork and harnessing collective strengths, individuals and organizations can unlock new avenues for financial success, proving that together, we can achieve far more than we ever could alone.

Adaptability in Action: Adjusting Financial Plans to Survive and Thrive

In the untamed world where wild dogs roam, adaptability is not just a trait; it's a survival instinct. These remarkable creatures have an innate ability to modify their hunting techniques, shifting strategies to match the ever-changing landscapes of their environment. This remarkable flexibility allows them to thrive, even when faced with the unexpected—a lesson that resonates deeply in the financial realm.

Financial markets, much like the wilderness, are dynamic and unpredictable. The ability to adapt one's financial strategies in response to changing conditions is crucial for success. For instance, an investor who diversifies their portfolio is embodying the wild dog's strategic approach to survival. Just as these animals hunt differently based on their surroundings, an investor must recognize when to pivot, exploring various asset classes or sectors to mitigate risks and seize new opportunities.

Consider the impact of market fluctuations on individual investments. When economic conditions shift—whether due to a recession, technological advancements, or regulatory changes—being adaptable means having the foresight to reassess and realign your financial strategies. This could involve reallocating funds, exploring alternative investments, or even developing new revenue streams. By staying attuned to market signals and responding proactively, individuals and businesses can safeguard their financial health and position themselves for growth, even in uncertain times.

Moreover, adaptability fosters resilience. Wild dogs demonstrate a remarkable ability to bounce back from setbacks, often regrouping and modifying their tactics when their initial plans falter. Similarly, financial setbacks—be it unexpected expenses, losses in investments, or shifts in income—should not deter one from pursuing their goals. Instead, they can be viewed as opportunities to reassess strategies and cultivate a more robust financial plan.

In a world that constantly demands agility, the ability to adapt is an invaluable asset. Embracing flexibility in financial planning ensures that individuals and organizations can navigate challenges with confidence, transforming potential obstacles into stepping stones toward greater success. Just as the wild dog thrives in a diverse and changing environment, so too can we flourish by harnessing the power of adaptability in our financial endeavours.

PERSEVERANCE PAYS: Staying Committed in the Face of Setbacks

In the vast expanse of the wild, wild dogs epitomize the spirit of perseverance. Their hunts are not short sprints; they are gruelling marathons that can stretch over several kilometres, requiring immense stamina and unwavering determination. These canines refuse to relent, tirelessly pursuing their prey with relentless focus. This same dedication serves as a powerful metaphor for the journey toward financial success.

Achieving financial goals—be it starting a business, building wealth, or planning for retirement—demands a level of commitment akin to that of the wild dog on the hunt. Challenges and setbacks are inevitable; just as wild dogs face obstacles in their pursuit, individuals often encounter financial hurdles such as unexpected expenses, market downturns, or changes in personal circumstances. However, it is during these difficult times that perseverance becomes most crucial.

Financial success is rarely a straight path. It requires resilience to navigate the winding roads and to confront adversity head-on. For instance, an entrepreneur may experience initial failures or face stiff competition, but those who remain steadfast, learning from their mistakes, are often the ones who eventually thrive. Similarly, investors may see their portfolios fluctuate, but those who hold firm, staying true to their long-term strategies rather than succumbing to panic, often reap the rewards when markets rebound.

The key lies in fostering a mindset of perseverance. It's about embracing the process rather than fixating solely on the outcome. Just as wild dogs do not abandon the chase after a single setback, individuals should adopt a long-term perspective, recognizing that consistent efforts will yield results over time. Celebrating small victories along the way can help maintain motivation and commitment, reinforcing the understanding that every step forward, no matter how small, is a move toward greater financial achievement.

In a world that often demands instant gratification, the tenacity displayed by wild dogs serves as a reminder of the value of persistence. Their success does not come from speed but from a steadfast commitment to their goal. By embodying this principle in our financial endeavours, we can cultivate a path toward success that withstands the test of time. Perseverance pays; it transforms dreams into realities, proving that dedication in the face of adversity is the true hallmark of financial triumph.

THE RESILIENCE FACTOR: Bouncing Back from Financial Challenges

In the wild, resilience is the lifeblood of the wild dog. These remarkable creatures are adept at overcoming adversity, displaying an unwavering ability to bounce back from challenges. Whether it's enduring a failed hunt or recovering from injuries, wild dogs exemplify the essence of resilience. This powerful trait serves as a vital lesson for individuals and businesses navigating the tumultuous landscape of personal finance and economic fluctuations.

Financial resilience is the capacity to recover from setbacks—losses, unexpected expenses, or downturns in the market—without losing sight of long-term goals. Just as wild dogs adapt their hunting strategies based on the environment and circumstances individuals must also adjust their financial strategies to weather storms. For instance, during an economic downturn, businesses might reassess their budgets, streamline operations, or pivot to new revenue streams to sustain themselves.

Building resilience in finance starts with a proactive approach to risk management. By creating a robust financial plan that includes an emergency fund, diversified investments, and insurance coverage, individuals and businesses can prepare themselves for unforeseen challenges. This safety net acts as a cushion, allowing them to absorb shocks without derailing their overall financial health.

Moreover, cultivating a growth mindset is crucial for fostering resilience. Instead of viewing setbacks as insurmountable obstacles, those who embrace challenges as opportunities for learning and growth are more likely to recover successfully. Just as wild dogs regroup and strategize after a missed opportunity, individuals can benefit from analysing their past financial decisions, learning from mistakes, and adapting their approach moving forward.

A prime example of resilience can be seen in individuals who have faced bankruptcy or significant financial loss. Many use these experiences as catalysts for change, refocusing their efforts and rebuilding their financial standing stronger than before. By developing new skills, seeking mentorship, or pursuing further education, they not only recover but often achieve greater success than they initially thought possible.

Ultimately, the lesson from wild dogs is clear: resilience is not just about enduring hardships; it's about bouncing back with renewed vigor and determination. Financial setbacks are a part of the journey, but with the right strategies and mindset, individuals can navigate through challenges and emerge stronger. Just as the wild dog perseveres through the hardships of the hunt, so too can we cultivate resilience, allowing us to reclaim our footing and continue our pursuit of financial stability and growth.

THE STRENGTH OF UNITY: Collective Power in Achieving Financial Goals

In the vast landscapes where the wild dog roams, one principle stands out as the cornerstone of their success: unity. These social animals showcase an extraordinary ability to work together, using their collective strength to hunt, defend, and thrive. Their teamwork not only enhances their hunting prowess but also serves as a powerful metaphor for achieving financial goals.

When individuals or organizations come together with a shared vision, they can tap into a wealth of resources, skills, and perspectives that far exceed what any single entity could achieve alone. This collective power is evident in various contexts—whether it's family finances, business partnerships, or investment groups. By aligning their goals and pooling their strengths, groups can navigate financial challenges more effectively and unlock greater opportunities.

Consider a family unit managing their finances. When family members communicate openly about their financial aspirations, they can work together to create a budget that reflects shared priorities. This unity in financial planning allows them to save for a family vacation, invest in education, or build a robust emergency fund. By holding each other accountable and celebrating milestones together, they cultivate a strong sense of teamwork that enhances their financial well-being.

In the business world, partnerships often drive innovation and growth. Strategic alliances allow companies to leverage each other's strengths, share resources, and minimize risks. For instance, a startup might collaborate with an established firm to access new markets or technology, resulting in a win-win situation. Just as wild dogs coordinate their hunting efforts, businesses can achieve collective success through synergy and collaboration.

Investment groups also exemplify the power of unity in the financial realm. By pooling capital, investors can access opportunities that may be out of reach individually, such as real estate ventures or startup investments. This collaborative approach not only diversifies risk but also fosters shared learning and decision-making. Group members can benefit from each other's insights, leading to more informed investment choices.

Furthermore, the sense of unity and camaraderie within a group enhances motivation and perseverance. When challenges arise—be it market downturns or unexpected expenses—working together fosters resilience. Members can encourage one another, share strategies for overcoming obstacles, and remain focused on their collective goals.

Ultimately, the wild dog serves as a powerful reminder that success is often a team effort. Embracing unity in financial pursuits—whether in family dynamics, business partnerships, or investment groups—can significantly enhance the likelihood of achieving goals. As wild dogs exemplify through their seamless cooperation, the strength of unity lies in its ability to harness diverse talents, share the burdens of challenges, and celebrate the triumphs together.

The Wild Dog's Legacy of Collaboration and Resilience

In the intricate tapestry of the animal kingdom, the wild dog stands out as a beacon of collaboration, adaptability, and relentless determination. Through their coordinated hunting strategies, they demonstrate the immense power of unity, illustrating that when individuals come together with a common purpose, they can achieve extraordinary results. Their ability to adapt to changing circumstances and persist through challenges serves as a vital lesson for anyone navigating the unpredictable waters of finance.

As we reflect on the remarkable qualities of these social hunters, we are reminded that financial success is rarely a solitary journey. Just as wild dogs rely on their pack for support, encouragement, and strength, individuals and businesses must also recognize the value of collaboration. Whether forming strategic alliances, sharing insights within a family unit, or pooling resources in investment groups, the collective power of unity can drive remarkable outcomes.

Moreover, the wild dog teaches us that resilience is essential in the face of adversity. Challenges are inevitable in both nature and finance, yet it is our response to these setbacks that truly defines us. By embracing flexibility, fostering teamwork, and remaining committed to our goals, we can bounce back from difficulties and continue our pursuit of financial growth.

In the end, let the wild dog's legacy inspire us to cultivate a spirit of collaboration and resilience in our own financial journeys. As we work together, adapt to challenges, and support one another, we unlock the potential for greater achievements. With the lessons learned from these remarkable creatures, we can navigate the complexities of the financial landscape with confidence, purpose, and a commitment to collective success.

Chapter 9: Elephant – The Giants of Financial Wisdom

In the world of finance, much like in the natural kingdom, there is no greater symbol of wisdom, strength, and resilience than the elephant. Towering over its environment, the elephant is not only a creature of immense power but also of profound intelligence and emotional depth. Known for their long memories and close-knit family structures, elephants represent the balance between brute strength and gentle leadership. These majestic giants can navigate vast terrains, adapting to different climates and challenges, just as financially astute individuals must learn to navigate the ever-changing economic landscape.

Elephants never forget—this isn't just an old saying; it's a testament to their extraordinary ability to learn from experience and pass down knowledge through generations. In the financial realm, this mirrors the importance of learning from past mistakes, gathering insights, and building on experiences to ensure a stable and prosperous future. An elephant's journey is long and arduous, but it moves with purpose, aware of the terrain and its surroundings. Likewise, building wealth and securing financial independence is not about quick sprints but a marathon of steady, well-calculated steps.

As this chapter unfolds, we'll delve into key financial lessons drawn from the remarkable characteristics of elephants—their patience, adaptability, and the unwavering strength they bring to protecting their herd. Whether it's their ability to store energy and water for harsh times or the way they leverage their size to protect their young, the elephant's every move holds a lesson in long-term financial planning, sustainability, and resilience.

Prepare to harness the wisdom of these giants, as we explore how to navigate financial challenges with foresight, defend your wealth, and ensure the security of future generations. Just like the elephant's legacy is built over decades, so too is the path to financial greatness—by balancing power with wisdom, and strength with careful planning.

PATIENCE IN WEALTH-Building: The Art of Long-Term Financial Planning

Elephants are renowned for their wisdom, patience, and the long-lasting bonds they form throughout their lives. Living in herds, they move with a sense of calm deliberation, covering vast distances over time. Their journey is not rushed, but purposeful, ensuring that the herd is protected and that the younger generations learn the ways of survival. This lifestyle of slow, steady progress mirrors a key principle in financial success: the importance of patience and long-term planning.

When it comes to building wealth, much like an elephant's gradual journey through life, financial growth is rarely instantaneous. Elephants don't sprint to their destinations, and similarly, wealth accumulation doesn't happen overnight. The most successful financial plans are those grounded in long-term thinking, where patience becomes an essential virtue. Whether it's saving for retirement, investing in stocks, or building generational wealth, it's the steady, persistent effort over time that yields the greatest results.

Take the example of retirement savings. For most people, the path to financial independence in retirement is a long-term journey. Contributions to a retirement account may seem small at first, but over the years, with the power of compound interest, those contributions grow significantly. Just as elephants rely on their long-term survival instincts, financial success requires individuals to have the foresight and patience to stick to their investment strategy, even when the rewards aren't immediate.

Warren Buffett, one of the world's most successful investors, embodies this elephant-like patience in his financial approach. Buffett is famous for his belief in long-term value investing, avoiding the temptation of short-term gains. His strategy is akin to the elephant's way of moving—slow and calculated but deeply focused on the long-term horizon. This patience, combined with disciplined investment, has allowed him to amass tremendous wealth over time, much like how elephants build their strength and presence gradually as they grow older and wiser.

In financial planning, patience goes hand in hand with delayed gratification. In a world where instant rewards are often desired, those who, like the elephant, can take a step back, view the bigger picture, and plan are often the ones who thrive. Sacrificing short-term indulgences—whether it's resisting unnecessary purchases or avoiding risky, high-stakes investments—can pave the way for greater financial stability and growth down the line.

The elephant's lifestyle teaches us that the journey to financial success is not a race. It's about moving forward with deliberate intent, embracing the slow but steady march toward financial independence. Just as an elephant safeguards its herd and ensures the future of its offspring, sound financial planning protects and nurtures future wealth, offering stability for generations to come.

In the financial world, patience truly is power. The ability to wait, to trust the process, and to think long-term separates those who merely survive from those who thrive. Whether it's saving for retirement or investing in assets that take time to appreciate, learning to think and act with the patience of an elephant can be the key to building enduring wealth and financial security.

ADAPTING TO CHANGING Environments: Flexibility in Financial Strategies

Elephants, despite their massive size, are remarkably adaptable creatures. Whether in savannas, forests, or deserts, they adjust to their surroundings, changing their behaviours and diet to thrive in different environments. This adaptability is crucial for their survival as they navigate changing weather conditions, food availability, and threats. Similarly, in the financial world, adaptability is one of the most important traits for achieving long-term success. Just as elephants adjust to shifting landscapes, individuals and businesses must be flexible with their financial strategies to survive and grow in ever-changing economic conditions.

In the investment world, adaptability means knowing when to revise strategies and pivot when necessary. Economic downturns, market volatility, or sudden changes in a specific industry are inevitable. The investors and businesses that thrive in the face of such shifts are those that remain open to change. For example, during the global financial crisis of 2008, many companies collapsed, but some adapted their strategies, cutting unnecessary expenses, shifting their focus to more resilient markets, or finding new ways to serve their customers. These businesses, much like elephants in a drought-stricken region, found ways to survive despite the challenges.

Consider the case of Netflix, which began as a DVD rental company but pivoted to streaming as it recognized the shift in how people consumed entertainment. This adaptability has kept the company ahead of its competition and allowed it to grow into one of the most dominant players in the entertainment industry. The lesson here is that flexibility isn't about changing directions constantly but about knowing when to adapt your strategy to reflect a changing environment.

Adaptable financial strategies also apply to personal finance. Whether it's navigating career changes, dealing with unexpected expenses, or adjusting savings and investment goals in response to life changes, being open to financial flexibility is key. For instance, individuals nearing retirement may need to rebalance their investment portfolios, shifting away from riskier assets like stocks to safer options like bonds, in response to market conditions or personal financial needs. This flexibility in strategy ensures that one's financial goals remain on track, regardless of external factors.

Similarly, small business owners must be able to adapt their financial strategies to changing market demands. During the COVID-19 pandemic, many businesses had to pivot rapidly—restaurants shifted to delivery services, and brick-and-mortar stores turned to e-commerce. Those who were flexible and quick to adapt not only survived but often found new opportunities to grow, while others, unwilling or unable to change, struggled.

Elephants know when to conserve energy and resources when times are tough and when to take advantage of an abundant environment. Financially, this translates into knowing when to cut back on spending or take calculated risks in more favourable conditions. Flexibility, like adaptability in nature, is a survival skill.

Financial success isn't just about sticking to one rigid plan. Like elephants, who change their patterns to thrive in different ecosystems, those who adjust their financial strategies based on changing market trends, economic conditions, or personal circumstances are more likely to find long-term success. Embracing financial flexibility allows for both survival during tough times and growth during times of abundance.

UNWAVERING STRENGTH: Building a Solid Financial Foundation

Elephants, revered for their formidable strength, epitomize the essence of stability and resilience in the wild. Their physical prowess allows them to traverse rugged terrains and confront predators, but their social structures add another layer of strength, as they support one another within tight-knit herds. This combination of physical and communal strength serves as a powerful metaphor for the importance of establishing a solid financial foundation in our own lives.

At the core of financial security lies the concept of building a robust foundation, which involves creating an emergency fund, managing debt effectively, and implementing risk management strategies. Much like an elephant standing its ground against a threat, having a well-prepared financial base provides the stability needed to withstand unexpected economic challenges.

Creating an emergency fund is one of the first steps toward financial security. This fund acts as a safety net, providing a cushion against unforeseen expenses such as medical emergencies, car repairs, or job loss. Just as elephants rely on their strong family bonds for support, individuals and families can find security in knowing they have resources to draw upon during tough times. A well-funded emergency reserve can mean the difference between weathering a financial storm or being swept away by it.

In addition to saving for emergencies, managing debt is crucial for maintaining financial stability. Elephants are known to carry the weight of their tusks and the responsibilities of their herds. In a similar vein, individuals must be mindful of their financial burdens. High levels of debt can be crippling, just as a weakened elephant struggles to navigate its environment. By prioritizing debt repayment and minimizing high-interest obligations, individuals can liberate themselves from financial constraints, allowing them to focus on building wealth and achieving long-term goals.

Moreover, managing risk is essential for a strong financial foundation. Just as elephants face various threats in the wild, such as poachers or habitat loss, individuals and businesses must also navigate risks that can jeopardize their financial well-being. This can include market fluctuations, economic downturns, or unforeseen expenses. By diversifying investments, obtaining appropriate insurance, and creating contingency plans, one can fortify their financial position against potential setbacks. For example, a well-diversified investment portfolio can help mitigate the risks associated with market volatility, just as an elephant benefit from the protection of its herd.

The importance of financial education cannot be overstated. Elephants are intelligent creatures that learn from experience and rely on the wisdom of older members of their herd. Similarly, individuals should seek knowledge about personal finance, investments, and risk management. By equipping oneself with financial literacy, one can make informed decisions that strengthen their financial foundation and prepare for a stable future.

Ultimately, the unwavering strength of elephants serves as a reminder of the power of a solid financial foundation. Just as these majestic animals stand firm in the face of adversity, individuals who prioritize financial security through effective saving, debt management, and risk mitigation can build resilience in their financial lives. Establishing a robust financial base is not merely a precaution; it is an investment in long-term stability and growth, ensuring that one can withstand economic storms and thrive in the years to come.

WISDOM IN FINANCIAL Decisions: Learning from Experience

In the vast and intricate landscapes where elephants roam, their remarkable memory and keen understanding of their environment play a vital role in their survival. These majestic creatures possess an innate wisdom gained through years of experience, allowing them to navigate the challenges of their habitat with grace and foresight. This wisdom, cultivated over time, serves as a powerful reminder of the importance of learning from our financial experiences—whether they be triumphs or setbacks.

Just as elephants rely on their memories to find food, water, and safe passage, individuals must learn to reflect on their past financial decisions to enhance their future choices. Financial wisdom is not merely about knowing what to do; it is about understanding the consequences of our actions and making informed decisions based on that knowledge. For instance, an investor who recalls a previous market downturn may approach new investments with a more cautious and diversified strategy, thus minimizing potential risks.

One key aspect of this journey is learning from financial mistakes. Just as elephants may encounter obstacles in their paths, individuals often face setbacks in their financial lives, such as impulsive spending, poor investment choices, or insufficient savings. Instead of viewing these mistakes as failures, they can be reframed as valuable lessons. For example, someone who invested heavily in a single stock that plummeted might now recognize the importance of diversification and implement that knowledge in future investments. This shift in perspective transforms past missteps into stepping stones for growth.

Moreover, informed decision-making is a hallmark of financial wisdom. Elephants are known to assess their surroundings, evaluating the best paths to take based on previous experiences. Similarly, individuals can benefit from gathering information, seeking advice, and analysing their financial situations before making significant decisions. This might involve consulting with financial advisors, reading about investment strategies, or participating in workshops. By actively engaging in learning and reflection, individuals can develop a well-rounded understanding of their finances, leading to more strategic choices.

Leveraging financial wisdom also involves understanding market trends and economic conditions. Just as elephants adapt their behaviours based on the seasons and availability of resources, individuals should remain attuned to shifts in the financial landscape. For instance, a person might notice a trend toward sustainable investing and decide to align their portfolio with socially responsible companies, reflecting their values while also capitalizing on emerging opportunities.

Finally, mentorship and community support play a crucial role in fostering financial wisdom. Just as young elephants learn from the matriarchs of their herds, individuals can benefit from engaging with mentors or financial groups that share knowledge and insights. These connections can provide guidance, encouragement, and accountability, ultimately enhancing one's financial journey.

The wisdom embodied by elephants serves as a powerful reminder that our past experiences—both good and bad—are essential building blocks for financial success. By embracing the lessons learned from our financial journeys, making informed decisions, and continually seeking knowledge, we can navigate the complex world of finance with confidence and clarity. Like elephants forging their paths through the wild, individuals who harness the power of financial wisdom can create a prosperous and secure future.

THE POWER OF LEGACY: Creating Wealth that Endures

In the intricate social structures of elephant herds, a profound sense of family and legacy pervades their existence. These magnificent creatures not only nurture their young but also impart invaluable knowledge and wisdom, ensuring that lessons learned throughout their lives are passed down to the next generation.

This deep-rooted sense of legacy serves as a powerful analogy for individuals seeking to create enduring wealth that benefits not only themselves but also their descendants.

Building a financial legacy begins with the understanding that wealth is not merely a personal asset; it is a tool that can empower future generations. Just as elephants work together to ensure the survival of their young, individuals can adopt a mindset focused on generational wealth. This means making deliberate financial choices that prioritize long-term stability and growth, allowing one's wealth to flourish over time. For instance, parents who invest in a diversified portfolio not only secure their financial future but also set a strong foundation for their children, enabling them to inherit a thriving asset base.

Estate planning is a crucial component of creating a legacy. Elephants often utilize their knowledge of migratory routes and resources, ensuring their young are well-equipped to thrive in their environment. Similarly, individuals can take proactive steps to plan their estates, outlining how their assets will be distributed after their passing. This can involve establishing trusts, creating wills, and engaging in conversations with family members about financial expectations and responsibilities. By doing so, individuals can prevent potential conflicts and ensure that their wealth is managed according to their values and intentions, much like elephants guiding their offspring through the complexities of life.

Moreover, wise investments play a pivotal role in the creation of generational wealth. Elephants are known to nurture their young, teaching them the skills needed to thrive in the wild. In the financial realm, this translates to investing in opportunities that will yield long-term benefits. Individuals can consider investments in real estate, stocks, or businesses that align with their values and vision for the future. By fostering an investment strategy that prioritizes growth and sustainability, one can build a robust financial legacy that stands the test of time.

Education also plays a significant role in creating a legacy. Elephants are known for their intelligence and ability to learn from their experiences, and similarly, individuals should focus on educating their children about financial literacy. Teaching them the principles of saving, investing, and managing money empowers the next generation to make informed financial decisions. For example, a family might establish a "financial education fund" to cover courses or workshops that teach their children essential financial skills, ensuring they are equipped to manage the wealth passed down to them.

Finally, cultivating a mindset of generosity can further enhance the legacy one leaves behind. Elephants often exhibit altruistic behaviours within their herds, demonstrating the importance of community and support. By incorporating philanthropy into financial planning, individuals can create a legacy that positively impacts society while also benefiting future generations. Establishing charitable foundations or contributing to causes that align with one's values not only enriches the lives of others but also instils a sense of purpose and responsibility in descendants.

The power of legacy, embodied by the family-oriented nature of elephants, underscores the importance of creating wealth that endures. By focusing on generational wealth, engaging in thoughtful estate planning, making wise investments, educating future generations, and fostering a spirit of generosity, individuals can build a financial legacy that thrives long after they are gone. Just as elephants traverse vast landscapes, passing on their wisdom and nurturing the next generation, so too can individuals leave behind a legacy that empowers and enriches the lives of those who follow.

The Enduring Legacy of Financial Wisdom

In the intricate tapestry of financial legacy, the lessons drawn from elephants illuminate the profound impact of patience, wisdom, and foresight. Just as these majestic creatures embody strength and nurturing, individuals can cultivate their financial legacies through deliberate planning and strategic decision-making. By embracing long-term financial strategies, adapting to changing environments, and prioritizing education and philanthropy, one can create a wealth foundation that not only sustains their family but also enriches future generations. The journey of building a lasting financial legacy requires a commitment to perseverance and a deep understanding of the value of time and patience. As individuals strive to emulate the enduring qualities of elephants, they can ensure their wealth serves as a powerful force for good, fostering stability, growth, and empowerment for generations to come. The legacy of financial wisdom, much like the memories of elephants, can echo through time, leaving a lasting impact on the lives it touches.

Chapter Ten: Leopard – The Art of Stealth and Precision in Finance

In the vast expanse of the wilderness, the leopard emerges as a master of stealth and precision, embodying the essence of adaptability and cunning. With its distinctive coat blending seamlessly into the dappled shadows of the savannah, the leopard is not just a predator; it's an artist of survival, leveraging its surroundings to stalk and secure its prey. Each graceful movement speaks to a strategy meticulously crafted through experience and instinct, where patience and timing are as critical as strength.

As we delve into the world of the leopard, we uncover valuable lessons for the financial realm. Just like this enigmatic creature, successful individuals and businesses navigate their financial journeys with a blend of strategy, adaptability, and an acute awareness of their environment. In a landscape fraught with challenges, those who embody the leopard's principles can thrive, making calculated moves that lead to triumph in their financial endeavours.

Prepare to explore the depths of financial stealth, learn the art of precision in investments, and discover how the leopard's timeless wisdom can guide you in securing your financial future. Embrace the allure of the hunt, where every decision is deliberate, every opportunity is seized, and the reward is not just survival but a flourishing legacy. Welcome to the world of the leopard—where the art of finance is a dance of elegance and strategy.

STEALTH AND PRECISION: The Importance of Targeted Investments

In the wild, the leopard epitomizes stealth, moving with an uncanny grace that allows it to blend into its surroundings. When hunting, it doesn't simply charge into the fray; instead, it observes, strategizes, and strikes with precision. This approach to hunting offers a powerful metaphor for investing: targeted investments require careful consideration, patience, and a clear understanding of one's financial goals.

When investors emulate the leopard's stealth, they focus on identifying specific opportunities that align with their financial aspirations. Rather than spreading their resources thin across a wide array of assets, they prioritize quality over quantity. Just as a leopard chooses its prey based on its strengths and the conditions of the hunt, so too should investors select assets that resonate with their strategic objectives.

For instance, consider the case of an investor looking to grow their wealth through real estate. Instead of purchasing multiple properties in various locations with little research, a savvy investor might opt to focus on a single property in a high-demand area that promises substantial rental yields. This targeted investment approach can yield greater returns, allowing for a more manageable and efficient allocation of resources.

Moreover, focusing on targeted investments allows individuals to leverage their expertise and insights. Much like a leopard utilizes its keen senses to navigate its environment, informed investors use market research and data analysis to home in on high-potential opportunities. This level of scrutiny not only minimizes risk but also enhances the chances of success in achieving financial goals.

Ultimately, the key takeaway from the leopard's hunting strategy is clear: targeted investments—characterized by stealth and precision—lead to more favourable outcomes in the financial landscape. By narrowing their focus and being strategic in their asset selection, investors can create a robust portfolio that stands resilient against market volatility, much like the leopard that thrives in the wild through its calculated manoeuvres. Embrace the art of stealthy investment and watch your financial aspirations come to fruition.

STALKING SUCCESS: DEVELOPING Effective Financial Strategies

In the stillness of the African wilderness, a leopard exemplifies patience as it stalks its prey, moving silently through the underbrush. Every inch it covers is deliberate, calculated, and steeped in strategy. This meticulous approach isn't just a testament to the leopard's hunting prowess; it also serves as a compelling metaphor for developing effective financial strategies.

To achieve financial success, one must embody the qualities of the leopard—planning and preparation are paramount. Just as a leopard invests time in understanding the behaviour and patterns of its prey, individuals and businesses should dedicate themselves to thorough research and analysis of the financial landscape. This means diving deep into market trends, examining economic indicators, and understanding the intricacies of investment options. Knowledge is the bedrock of informed decision-making.

For example, consider an entrepreneur looking to launch a new product. Instead of rushing to market, a prudent approach mirrors that of the leopard: conduct market research, identify consumer needs, and analyse competitors. By taking the time to develop a comprehensive business strategy, the entrepreneur can position their product for maximum impact, increasing the likelihood of success.

Timing is another critical element in stalking success. Just as the leopard knows when to make its move—waiting for the perfect moment to pounce—financial decisions should not be made impulsively. In investing, waiting for the right opportunity can mean the difference between success and failure. By staying attuned to market fluctuations and economic conditions, investors can seize the moment when conditions are favourable, maximizing their returns.

In the world of finance, success favours the patient and the prepared. By developing strategic financial plans grounded in research and analysis, individuals can navigate their financial journeys with purpose and precision. Much like a leopard stalking its prey, calculated moves lead to substantial rewards. Embrace this strategic mindset, and you too can achieve your financial goals, one well-timed decision at a time.

ACUTE AWARENESS: STAYING Informed in the Financial Jungle

In the dense tapestry of the African wilderness, a leopard moves with an acute awareness of its surroundings. Every rustle in the grass, every flicker of movement, is noted with precision. This heightened sense of awareness is not merely a survival instinct; it's a critical strategy that can be applied to the realm of finance. In the fast-paced world of investments and economic shifts, staying informed is paramount for success.

Being financially savvy requires more than just basic knowledge; it demands an ongoing commitment to understanding the intricate web of market dynamics. Just as the leopard relies on its senses to detect changes in its environment, individuals and businesses must cultivate a keen awareness of economic conditions, market fluctuations, and emerging trends. This involves actively monitoring news, engaging with financial reports, and following industry developments.

For instance, imagine an investor who keeps a pulse on the technology sector. By staying informed about advancements and changes within this rapidly evolving industry, the investor can identify promising startups or emerging technologies poised for growth. This acute awareness allows them to make timely investments, leveraging opportunities that others might overlook.

Moreover, awareness extends beyond mere observation; it involves analyzing the implications of changes within the market. Economic indicators, such as inflation rates, interest rates, and unemployment figures, can significantly impact investment choices. Just as a leopard assesses its surroundings before making a move, individuals must evaluate how these factors influence their financial landscape.

In the financial jungle, those who maintain vigilance and stay informed are better equipped to navigate uncertainty. They can pivot in response to shifts, seize opportunities, and mitigate risks. By adopting a mindset of continuous learning and awareness, you can empower yourself to make informed decisions that align with your financial goals.

Ultimately, the lesson from the leopard is clear: acute awareness is a vital asset in the journey toward financial success. By honing your ability to observe, analyze, and respond to the ever-changing financial environment, you position yourself not just as a participant but as a strategic player in the financial game. Embrace the instincts of the leopard, and let your awareness guide you to prosperity.

FACING CHALLENGES: Resilience in Overcoming Financial Obstacles

Leopards, despite their strength and agility, are not without challenges. Whether it's facing rival predators or enduring the harshness of shifting environments, they must constantly adapt and persevere. In the same way, the financial world is fraught with obstacles, from volatile markets to unforeseen economic downturns. Resilience, much like in the life of a leopard, becomes an indispensable trait for survival and success.

Financial resilience is about more than just weathering the storm; it's about thriving through adversity. A well-prepared investor, like a leopard braving the wilderness, anticipates challenges. Setbacks such as unexpected expenses, failed investments, or a declining market can shake one's financial stability. However, having a solid strategy in place allows for recovery and even growth after difficult periods.

Consider the 2008 financial crisis. Many investors saw their portfolios crumble under the weight of collapsing markets. But those who maintained a resilient mindset—who had diversified investments, emergency funds, and adaptable strategies—were able to endure the crisis and eventually rebuild their wealth. Like a leopard waiting for the right moment to reassert its dominance in a new territory, resilient individuals bounced back, positioning themselves for success as the markets rebounded.

Resilience also involves the ability to adapt to changing circumstances. Just as the leopard adjusts its hunting techniques when prey becomes scarce or environmental conditions shift, so must individuals pivot their financial strategies. This may mean altering investment portfolios, cutting unnecessary expenses, or seeking new income streams. The key is not to be discouraged by temporary setbacks, but to remain focused on the long-term financial goal.

In facing challenges, resilience is not just about holding ground; it's about learning and evolving through every obstacle. The most successful financial journeys are those where setbacks become stepping stones to greater financial wisdom and strength. Like the leopard, undeterred by its trials, a resilient financial mindset ensures that challenges are not the end of the road but a chance to reassess, adapt, and continue moving forward.

THE ART OF PATIENCE and Critical Thinking: Mastering the Financial Landscape

Leopards are masters of patience, often lying in wait for hours before making their decisive move. This skill of knowing when to act—and when to hold back—is one of the keys to their survival. Similarly, in the financial world, patience and critical thinking are essential for long-term success. Those who rush into investments without careful analysis or act impulsively are likely to miss out on better opportunities or, worse, face significant losses.

In finance, patience allows investors to wait for the right moment to make a move, just as a leopard waits for the opportune time to pounce. Whether it's waiting for the market to correct itself, holding on to long-term investments, or resisting the urge to make impulsive decisions based on market volatility, patience is a trait that separates successful investors from those who fall prey to short-term thinking. For instance, Warren Buffet, one of the greatest investors of all time, often speaks about the value of "sitting on cash" until the perfect opportunity arises. His ability to wait patiently for the right investments has played a major role in his financial success.

Critical thinking complements patience, allowing individuals to make sound financial decisions based on analysis, data, and strategy. Leopards rely on their sharp instincts and calculated planning to catch prey, and in the same way, financial decision-makers must rely on careful research and clear thinking. Evaluating market trends, analysing risks, and understanding the broader economic landscape are crucial skills for navigating the complexities of finance. It's not just about reacting to the present but about thinking several steps ahead and planning for the future.

For example, during economic downturns, rather than panicking and selling off assets, savvy investors with critical thinking skills might see it as an opportunity to buy undervalued stocks or real estate. By exercising patience and careful consideration, they position themselves for significant gains when the market recovers.

Mastering the financial landscape, like mastering the art of the hunt, requires both the patience to wait for the right moment and the critical thinking to ensure that when you do act, your move is calculated and precise. Through this balance of patience and strategy, you can make decisions that lead to long-term financial success, much like the leopard's perfectly timed strike that ensures its survival.

Chapter Eleven: Lion – The King of the Financial Jungle

The lion's roar echoes across the savannah, a sound that signals authority and demands respect. As the apex predator, the lion's dominance isn't just about raw power; it's also about its unmatched ability to strategize, conserve energy, and take precise, well-calculated actions. The lion doesn't waste time chasing every opportunity that presents itself. Instead, it waits—observing, assessing, and choosing only the moments when success is almost guaranteed. This mindset is what sets the lion apart, making it the ruler of the wild.

In the financial jungle, becoming a lion—someone who dominates the market with confidence and skill—requires similar traits. It's not about being the loudest or most aggressive but about cultivating a strong presence and a strategic mind. Lions don't rush; they act when they're sure the return on their effort will be worth it. The same principle applies to financial success—learning when to make bold moves, when to conserve resources, and when to strike with precision.

Transitioning from being a small player into the "big fish" of the financial jungle is a journey of growth, resilience, and sharp decision-making. It requires more than just ambition; it's about understanding the terrain of the market, recognizing opportunities, and being unafraid to assert your position. The lion teaches us that true dominance is built on a foundation of patience, confidence, and strength. By mastering these qualities, anyone can rise to the top of their financial game, earning not just wealth but influence and respect in the world of finance.

Becoming the lion of the financial world means knowing when to take risks, maintaining a sharp sense of awareness, and developing the confidence to lead in a competitive environment. Like the lion, who rules its territory with dignity and power, a financial leader understands that real success comes from mastering the art of balance—between boldness and patience, strategy and action, vision and execution.

This chapter will dive deep into the journey of transitioning from a captive, someone merely reacting to market forces, into a captor—one who shapes and leads financial outcomes. As we explore the lion's traits, we will uncover how anyone can evolve into a dominant force in their financial journey, mastering both the art of strategy and the discipline of patience. From stealthy execution to commanding respect in the market, this chapter will serve as a guide to unlocking your full potential.

COMMANDING YOUR TERRITORY: Establishing Your Financial Domain

In the wild, a lion's territory is its kingdom—a place it has marked, claimed, and fiercely defended. No other predator dares to cross its boundaries without the risk of confrontation. This territorial dominance allows the lion to control its resources, from waterholes to hunting grounds, ensuring that it has everything necessary for survival and success.

In the financial world, claiming your territory works in much the same way. Establishing your financial domain means staking your claim in the market by identifying where your strengths lie and focusing your efforts on building a solid foundation. Whether it's in personal finance, business, or investments, you must establish clear boundaries—deciding which assets to invest in, what sectors to focus on, and what risks you are willing to take. Just as a lion doesn't wander, you need a well-defined strategy that aligns with your long-term financial goals.

Once you've carved out your space, the next step is to defend it. This could mean safeguarding your investments through diversification, protecting your assets by building an emergency fund or ensuring your business's continued growth by reinvesting profits wisely. Commanding your territory also involves understanding the competition—knowing what other market players are doing and how you can stay ahead of the curve.

A real-world example of this can be seen in business moguls like Jeff Bezos, who established Amazon as an untouchable force in e-commerce. Bezos claimed his space by focusing on delivering an exceptional customer experience and building a robust logistics network. Over time, Amazon became the leader in its domain, outmanoeuvring competitors and maintaining dominance through innovation and strategic expansion.

For individuals, commanding your financial territory could mean setting up multiple streams of income—investing in stocks, real estate, or even starting a side business. The key is to protect and grow your wealth over time, ensuring that you're not just surviving but thriving, no matter what challenges arise.

In finance, your domain is your expertise, your investments, and your carefully curated portfolio. Once you've marked your territory, you must stay vigilant, just like the lion, ensuring that you continuously guard and expand your financial kingdom.

THE POWER OF THE PRIDE: Building Strategic Alliances

In the animal kingdom, lions are unique not just for their might but also for their social structure. They live in groups known as prides, which are typically made up of related females, their offspring, and a few dominant males. This social dynamic enhances their hunting success and ensures that the pride can defend its territory against intruders. The power of pride lies in cooperation, collaboration, and shared responsibility.

Translating this concept into the financial landscape, building strategic alliances can be a game-changer in achieving success. Just as lions work together to hunt and protect their territory, individuals and businesses can thrive by forming partnerships, collaborating with others, and creating networks that enhance their financial strength.

Strategic alliances can take many forms. For entrepreneurs, this might mean joining forces with complementary businesses to cross-promote products or share resources. For investors, collaborating with like-minded individuals to form investment clubs can provide collective insights and opportunities that might be unavailable when operating alone.

Consider the example of companies that engage in joint ventures. For instance, Starbucks partnered with PepsiCo to create ready-to-drink coffee beverages. By combining Starbucks' coffee expertise with PepsiCo's distribution power, both companies expanded their market reach and revenue streams. This collaboration allowed them to leverage each other's strengths, creating a win-win scenario that would have been challenging to achieve independently.

For individuals, think about how networking can lead to new opportunities. Building relationships with financial advisors, mentors, or industry peers can open doors to investments, job offers, or collaborative projects. Attending seminars, joining professional associations, or even participating in online communities can help expand your pride of allies, creating a supportive environment that fosters growth.

Just as a pride's strength lies in its members working together, your financial success will often depend on your ability to create and maintain strategic alliances. These connections can provide the necessary support, resources, and insights needed to navigate the complexities of the financial jungle.

EMBRACING THE THRILL of the Chase: Taking Calculated Risks

Lions are renowned for their prowess in hunting, which often requires a calculated approach. They don't simply rush headlong into a chase; instead, they analyze their surroundings, assess their prey, and choose the optimal moment to strike. This measured strategy maximizes their chances of success and minimizes unnecessary energy expenditure.

In the realm of finance, embracing the thrill of the chase translates to taking calculated risks. Just as lions evaluate their opportunities before making a move, investors and business leaders must assess potential risks and rewards before committing to financial decisions. This doesn't mean avoiding risk altogether—rather, it means approaching it with a well-thought-out strategy.

Taking calculated risks involves understanding your financial goals, market conditions, and the potential impacts of your decisions. For example, launching a new product line can be daunting, but with thorough market research, you can identify gaps in the market and position your offering effectively. This strategic approach allows you to invest resources wisely and increase the likelihood of a successful outcome.

Consider the story of a tech startup that decided to pivot its business model after initially focusing on one product. By researching emerging trends, they identified a growing demand for a different service. This decision involved risk—shifting focus meant reallocating funds and resources—but it ultimately led to exponential growth and market leadership. Their ability to embrace calculated risk paid off, demonstrating that sometimes the biggest rewards come from bold decisions backed by research and insight.

Additionally, being aware of when to take risks can set you apart from the competition. The financial landscape is ever-changing, with new opportunities arising regularly. Successful investors recognize these moments and are prepared to act decisively when the time is right. This involves not only being vigilant but also being ready to pivot strategies when needed.

The thrill of the chase in the financial world is not just about speed; it's about strategy, timing, and informed decision-making. By learning to assess risks carefully and embrace the calculated nature of financial endeavours, you can increase your chances of achieving significant rewards in your journey to becoming a big fish in the financial jungle.

UNITY IN THE PRIDE: The Power of Collaboration and Networking

Lions are not solitary hunters; they thrive in groups known as prides. This social structure is crucial for their survival and success. Working together allows them to take down larger prey and defend their territory more effectively than any individual could on their own. The strength of the pride lies in its unity, and this concept translates seamlessly into the financial world, where collaboration and networking are vital for achieving success.

In finance, the power of collaboration manifests through partnerships, alliances, and networking opportunities. Just as lions depend on one another for hunting and protection, individuals and businesses can leverage their connections to enhance their financial ventures. Collaborating with others allows for the pooling of resources, sharing of knowledge, and increased access to opportunities that may otherwise remain out of reach.

Consider a scenario where entrepreneurs join forces to create a co-working space. By pooling their resources, they can offer a shared environment that attracts a diverse clientele, fostering innovation and collaboration. This synergy leads to greater success than if each entrepreneur were to operate independently, as the combined efforts create a vibrant community that draws in new clients and enhances visibility.

Networking is another crucial aspect of collaboration in finance. Building relationships with others in your industry opens doors to valuable insights, mentorship, and potential partnerships. The connections you cultivate can lead to referrals, joint ventures, or even investment opportunities. Just as a lion pride itself on its strong bonds within the group, individuals who actively engage in networking can fortify their positions in the financial landscape.

Moreover, collaboration can extend beyond immediate circles. Engaging with diverse perspectives from various sectors can spark innovation and drive growth. For instance, a company that collaborates with tech startups may gain insights into emerging technologies that can streamline operations and improve efficiency. This willingness to connect and collaborate enables businesses to adapt and thrive in an ever-evolving financial environment.

In essence, the power of collaboration and networking in finance is akin to the unity within a lion pride. By embracing the strength found in relationships and partnerships, individuals can enhance their financial prospects and navigate the complexities of the financial jungle with greater success.

THE ROAR OF AUTHORITY: Establishing Your Presence in the Financial Jungle

Lions are known for their powerful roar, a sound that can travel several miles and serve as a declaration of their dominance in the savannah. This roar is not just a means of communication; it signifies their authority and presence within their territory. In the financial world, establishing a strong presence and asserting authority is crucial for success. This aspect focuses on how individuals can cultivate their brand, communicate effectively, and position themselves as leaders in their respective fields.

In finance, authority is often tied to expertise and reputation. Just as a lion's roar announces its strength, your personal or professional brand should convey confidence and competence. Building authority begins with mastering your craft, whether through education, experience, or continuous learning. The more knowledgeable and skilled you become, the more others will recognize your expertise, leading to opportunities for influence and leadership.

Consider the case of an investment advisor who consistently provides valuable insights and results for clients. By sharing knowledge through articles, seminars, or social media, they establish themselves as a trusted authority in the field. This visibility not only attracts new clients but also fosters loyalty among existing ones, as people naturally gravitate towards those they perceive as knowledgeable and credible.

Effective communication is another essential element of establishing authority. A lion's roar is unmistakable, and in the same vein, your voice should be clear and impactful. Whether you're presenting a business proposal, negotiating a deal, or sharing insights with your network, communicating confidently and assertively can significantly enhance your influence. This involves not only articulating your ideas well but also actively listening to others, showing that you value their perspectives.

Positioning yourself as a leader also involves being visible and approachable within your industry. Attend networking events, participate in industry forums, or engage in public speaking opportunities to showcase your expertise and connect with others. Just as lions claim their territory, establishing your presence in the financial landscape requires a proactive approach to visibility. The more you are seen and heard, the more likely you are to be regarded as an authority.

Furthermore, authority comes with the responsibility to lead and mentor others. Sharing your knowledge and helping others grow can enhance your reputation and solidify your position as a respected figure in your field. When you empower others, you not only contribute to their success but also elevate your standing within the community.

In the financial jungle, establishing your presence and asserting your authority is paramount. By mastering your craft, communicating effectively, and actively engaging with others, you can create a powerful brand that resonates with your audience. Just as the lion's roar commands respect and attention, your authority can open doors to opportunities and elevate your financial journey.

Chapter Twelve: Sunset – The Final Chapter of Financial Mastery

As the day draws to a close, the sun sets, casting its last golden light over the horizon. In the same way, financial journeys come full circle, bringing with them the culmination of years of hard work, careful planning, and disciplined execution. The sunset doesn't mark an end, but rather a beautiful transition—much like financial independence or the passing on of a legacy. It's the moment where all efforts converge, leading to the achievement of lifelong financial goals, be it retiring in comfort, ensuring wealth for future generations, or savoring the fruits of well-earned financial freedom.

In this final chapter, we will explore what it means to arrive at the sunset of your financial journey, and how to gracefully transition from a period of wealth-building to enjoying and sustaining that wealth. Just as the sun sets with grace and purpose, so too should your financial decisions in this stage reflect wisdom, security, and foresight.

The chapter will guide you through the mindset and strategies necessary to solidify your financial accomplishments, ensuring that you leave behind a lasting impact while enjoying the results of your hard work. It's not just about wealth preservation—it's about finding peace and fulfillment in your financial freedom and preparing for the legacy that will carry on long after the sun sets on your journey.

THE ART OF WEALTH PRESERVATION: Protecting What You've Built

As the sun begins to set on your financial journey, the focus naturally shifts from accumulation to preservation. Just as a long day ends with a calm, beautiful sunset, your financial life should transition into a phase where the primary goal is protecting and securing the wealth you've worked so hard to build. This stage is about safeguarding your assets and ensuring that they remain intact, not just for you, but for the generations to come.

In this theme, we'll explore strategies for wealth preservation, emphasizing the importance of a proactive approach to managing risks, liabilities, and unforeseen challenges. One key aspect of wealth preservation is **risk management**—ensuring that your financial portfolio is structured to minimize potential losses. This could involve diversifying your investments to avoid overexposure to any one market or sector, or it might mean shifting toward more conservative assets, such as bonds, that provide stability in uncertain times.

Another essential element is **asset protection**. As wealth increases, so does the need to shield it from potential threats, such as lawsuits, taxes, or even family disputes. Establishing legal frameworks like trusts or insurance policies can act as protective barriers, ensuring that your assets are shielded from unnecessary risks and legal complications.

Think of this phase as the financial equivalent of putting up defenses around your estate. You're no longer focused on expanding your kingdom; instead, you're solidifying your walls and strengthening the foundation that supports everything you've built. Much like seasoned investors who shift their focus to lower-risk investments or real estate, this period calls for deliberate, careful decision-making to avoid any setbacks that could threaten the wealth accumulated over time.

Real-World Example: Consider Warren Buffett's philosophy of wealth preservation. After decades of aggressive investing, Buffett emphasizes minimizing risks as his wealth has grown. By ensuring that his investments are stable and diversified, he focuses on steady growth and security rather than chasing high-risk returns. He's more focused on not losing money than on making it quickly—a core principle of wealth preservation.

Finally, it's important to recognize that wealth preservation also means **maintaining a disciplined financial lifestyle**. Many people, after reaching significant wealth, become tempted to engage in lavish spending or risky ventures. However, the key to true financial mastery lies in maintaining discipline, avoiding unnecessary extravagances, and continuing to live in a way that reflects long-term financial stability.

The sunset phase is not about slowing down completely, but rather about shifting priorities. It's about ensuring that your wealth lasts, supporting you through retirement, securing your legacy, and allowing you to enjoy the fruits of your labor without the fear of financial decline. It's a peaceful, strategic stage in which the primary goal is to preserve and protect, ensuring that everything you've worked for remains intact as you move into this next phase of life.

LEGACY AND WEALTH TRANSFER: Ensuring Your Financial Impact Lives On

As the sun sets on your active wealth-building journey, the focus naturally shifts toward the legacy you will leave behind. Legacy and wealth transfer represent the culmination of a lifetime of financial efforts, ensuring that what you've built not only sustains you but also benefits those who come after you. Much like the sunset marks the end of a day, it also symbolizes the passing of knowledge, resources, and influence on the next generation.

In this theme, we explore the importance of **planning your financial legacy**. Legacy is more than just money; it's the impact you leave on your family, your community, and even the broader world. A well-planned financial legacy ensures that your values, wisdom, and resources are transferred in a meaningful way that supports the long-term success of your heirs or chosen beneficiaries.

The core aspect of wealth transfer is **estate planning**—making sure your assets are distributed according to your wishes, minimizing taxes, and avoiding legal disputes. This may include creating wills, setting up trusts, and ensuring that your financial affairs are in order well before you pass on. An essential part of estate planning is reducing the tax burden on your beneficiaries, ensuring they receive the maximum benefit from your hard-earned wealth.

Generational wealth is another crucial component of this theme. Building a financial legacy involves teaching the next generation how to manage, grow, and preserve the wealth they inherit. It's about more than just leaving money behind; it's about leaving behind a framework for financial success. By instilling financial literacy and responsible wealth management practices in your heirs, you ensure that your legacy doesn't end with a transfer of assets but continues to grow and benefit future generations.

Real-World Example: One well-known figure who has focused extensively on generational wealth is Bill Gates. Through the Bill and Melinda Gates Foundation, he has structured his financial legacy not only for his family but for the world at large. His approach to legacy involves both wealth transfer and a clear vision for how that wealth will be used for positive global impact, ensuring that his financial resources continue to serve a purpose long after he's gone.

Another essential element in legacy planning is considering **philanthropy**. Many individuals use their wealth to support causes they care about, leaving behind a legacy of positive social impact. Whether through charitable donations, setting up foundations, or funding specific initiatives, philanthropy allows your wealth to create meaningful change in the world, ensuring that your life's work benefits others beyond your immediate circle.

In planning your legacy, you're also creating a sense of **emotional fulfillment**—the peace of knowing that your life's work will continue to influence others in positive ways. You'll be able to take comfort in the knowledge that your family is financially secure and that your principles and ideals will be carried forward through the institutions, people, or causes you've chosen to support.

Legacy and wealth transfer are the ultimate financial goals for many, a way of ensuring that the sunset of your financial life illuminates the path for those who follow. Through careful planning and thoughtful decision-making, you can ensure that what you've built over a lifetime not only lasts but continues to grow and serve others long after you're gone.

EMBRACING FINANCIAL Freedom: The Joy of Reaping the Rewards

As the sun begins to set on your wealth-building journey, a new phase emerges—one where the focus shifts from accumulating wealth to enjoying the fruits of your labor. This theme explores the concept of **financial freedom**, the stage where you can finally experience the joy and freedom that comes with years of careful planning, discipline, and patience. It's the culmination of your financial efforts, where you gain the autonomy to live life on your own terms, free from the constraints of daily financial worries.

Financial freedom isn't just about reaching a specific number in your bank account—it's about **having the flexibility to make choices that enrich your life**. Whether that means retiring early, traveling the world, pursuing passion projects, or spending more time with family, financial freedom gives you the power to shape your future without the constant pressure of earning more or working harder. It's about finding balance and fulfillment, allowing yourself to savor the rewards of your hard work.

Key Elements of Financial Freedom:

- **Passive income**: By the time you've achieved financial freedom, your money should be working for you. Through investments, real estate, or other income-generating assets, you've built a foundation where your wealth grows even without your active involvement. This income allows you to step back from the grind and focus on living a life of purpose and enjoyment.

- **Time freedom**: One of the most valuable aspects of financial freedom is gaining control over your time. Instead of trading hours for dollars, you have the luxury of deciding how to spend your days. Whether it's dedicating more time to family, personal development, or charitable causes, financial freedom allows you to prioritize what matters most to you.
- **Security and peace of mind**: Achieving financial freedom means reaching a point where you no longer have to worry about unexpected expenses, economic downturns, or job instability. You've built a financial safety net, including emergency funds and investments, that ensures your future is secure, even in the face of uncertainty.

Real-World Example: Consider Warren Buffett, who, despite being one of the wealthiest individuals in the world, lives a relatively modest lifestyle and enjoys the freedom that comes with financial independence. He uses his wealth strategically, not only to maintain his financial security but to pursue personal interests like philanthropy, mentoring, and investing in causes that align with his values. Buffett's financial freedom allows him to make decisions based on passion and impact rather than necessity.

Another inspiring example of financial freedom is author and entrepreneur Tim Ferriss. Through his book *The 4-Hour Workweek*, Ferriss emphasizes the importance of designing a lifestyle that prioritizes freedom over constant financial pursuit. He advocates for finding ways to generate passive income, delegating work, and focusing on quality of life—all key aspects of achieving financial freedom.

Ultimately, embracing financial freedom is about **celebrating the journey** you've taken to reach this point. It's about recognizing that you've earned the right to live life according to your desires, whether that means scaling back on work, spending more time with loved ones, or embarking on new adventures. Financial freedom gives you the confidence to pursue your passions, contribute to society in meaningful ways, and fully embrace the life you've always envisioned.

In this stage, the sunset symbolizes the transition from relentless pursuit to peaceful enjoyment—a time to reflect on your accomplishments and indulge in the satisfaction that comes from financial independence. It's a reminder that wealth is not just about accumulating assets but about creating the freedom to live the life you've always dreamed of.

PLANNING FOR THE INEVITABLE: Leaving a Financial Legacy

As the sunset of life draws near, it's essential to consider how your wealth and values will continue to impact others after you're gone. This theme centers on the importance of **estate planning and leaving a lasting financial legacy**. Much like an artist putting the finishing touches on a masterpiece, this phase focuses on ensuring that your hard-earned wealth and the lessons you've learned are passed down to future generations in a meaningful way.

Leaving a legacy is more than just distributing your assets—it's about **crafting a purposeful plan** that reflects your values, protects your loved ones, and continues to create positive change even after you're no longer around. It's a way of extending the influence of your financial journey, ensuring that the decisions you make today will continue to resonate tomorrow.

Key Aspects of Financial Legacy Planning:

- **Estate planning and wills**: A crucial step in legacy building is creating a will or estate plan that clearly outlines how your assets will be managed and distributed. By having a clear, legally binding document, you reduce the likelihood of disputes or confusion among family members, ensuring that your wealth goes to those you intend to benefit. **Estate planning allows you to maintain control over your assets** and ensure they are used in ways that align with your wishes.
- **Trusts and charitable giving**: For those looking to leave a lasting impact, setting up trusts or charitable foundations can be an effective way to ensure that your wealth is used for causes that matter to you. Many financially successful individuals, such as Bill Gates, have chosen to use their wealth not only to provide for their families but also to make a lasting difference in the world. Through the Bill and Melinda Gates Foundation, Gates has committed to using his fortune for global health, education, and poverty alleviation, reflecting his values even beyond his lifetime.
- **Passing down financial wisdom**: In addition to money, passing down **financial education** is an essential part of creating a legacy. It's not enough to leave assets behind—true legacy-building involves teaching the next generation how to manage and grow wealth responsibly. This can involve everything from basic budgeting lessons

to more advanced investment strategies, ensuring that your heirs are equipped with the knowledge and skills to carry on your financial philosophy.

- **Tax efficiency**: A well-structured legacy plan should consider the tax implications of transferring wealth. With careful planning, it's possible to minimize estate taxes and ensure that more of your wealth goes to your intended beneficiaries rather than being eroded by government taxes. This includes strategies like **gifting during your lifetime**, setting up family trusts, or utilizing tax-efficient investment vehicles.

Real-World Example: A great example of legacy planning comes from Oprah Winfrey, who has built a multi-billion-dollar empire. Beyond her personal wealth, Oprah has taken significant steps to ensure her impact will continue through charitable giving and her foundations. By investing in education, she aims to create long-term change in communities worldwide, leaving a legacy that extends far beyond her career.

Another notable case is the Rockefeller family, whose wealth has transcended generations. John D. Rockefeller, one of the wealthiest men in history, not only built an empire but also instilled in his descendants the values of philanthropy, financial responsibility, and wealth preservation. His legacy lives on, with the Rockefeller Foundation continuing to contribute to important causes, from education to environmental conservation.

Preparing for the future is an act of responsibility and foresight. Just as the sunset signals the end of one day and the preparation for the next, planning for your legacy ensures that your life's work will continue to benefit others long after you are gone.

Whether through supporting your loved ones, creating charitable foundations, or passing down the lessons you've learned, leaving a legacy allows you to contribute to the world in a meaningful and lasting way.

By planning ahead and making strategic decisions now, you can ensure that your financial story does not end with you but continues to empower and inspire future generations.

REFLECTING ON THE JOURNEY: Wisdom Gained Along the Financial Path

As the sun sets on any journey, it brings an opportunity for reflection—an essential part of growth and understanding. This final theme focuses on the importance of **looking back at your financial journey**, acknowledging both your successes and setbacks, and **extracting the lessons** that will guide future decisions. Just as the colours of the sunset signal the close of a day, reflection allows you to see the full spectrum of your financial life, putting everything into perspective.

Reflection is not only about celebrating milestones or overcoming obstacles; it's about **acknowledging how far you've come** and gaining clarity on where you want to go next. Financial success is rarely a straight line, and looking back on the twists and turns helps to shape the wisdom you carry forward. This wisdom—gained through experience—becomes your most valuable asset as you continue to navigate new opportunities and challenges.

Key Aspects of Financial Reflection:

- **Assessing long-term goals**: Just as a sunset allows us to appreciate the day that has passed, reflection gives us the chance to assess how our long-term financial goals have evolved. Have you stayed on track with the goals you set earlier in your financial journey? If not, reflection helps you recalibrate, understanding which goals still align with your vision and which may need adjustment.
- **Learning from past mistakes**: Mistakes are an inevitable part of any financial journey, but reflection allows us to turn those mistakes into valuable lessons. Whether it was a poor investment decision, overspending, or not saving enough, the ability to reflect on those choices and **learn from them** is what separates financially savvy individuals from those who repeat the same errors. The greatest investors—such as Warren Buffett—acknowledge that mistakes are part of the process and often lead to deeper insights and smarter decisions.
- **Celebrating successes**: Reflection is also about recognizing what went right celebrating the milestones and achievements that have moved you closer to your financial goals. Whether it's paying off debt, reaching a savings target, or securing a long-term investment, acknowledging these victories boosts confidence and reminds you of your ability to overcome challenges. These successes can serve as motivation for future endeavours, reinforcing the habits and strategies that have proven effective.
- **Gaining perspective**: The process of reflecting gives you the opportunity to **gain perspective on your financial**

journey. Sometimes, when caught in the day-to-day grind of managing finances, it's easy to lose sight of the bigger picture. Reflection helps you zoom out and see the larger story—how every choice, every risk, and every achievement has contributed to your growth. This perspective is essential for maintaining focus on your ultimate financial vision and understanding that each decision plays a part in the broader landscape of your wealth-building journey.

- **Carrying wisdom forward**: Just as the sun sets each day with the promise of a new dawn, reflection is not an endpoint but rather a **starting point for future success.** The wisdom you gain from reflection becomes the foundation for your next chapter, informing smarter decisions, deeper financial strategies, and better risk management. This wisdom can be passed down to others, whether it's family, friends, or future generations, creating a ripple effect that extends beyond your own life.

Real-World Example: One example of the power of reflection is Ray Dalio, founder of Bridgewater Associates, one of the largest hedge funds in the world. Dalio credits much of his success to reflecting on his failures and mistakes, using those experiences to shape his investment philosophy. He famously documents his reflections and principles, which have not only helped him grow as an investor but have also become a guide for others seeking financial success. His approach underscores the value of reflecting on both successes and setbacks, extracting key lessons to carry forward.

Similarly, Oprah Winfrey's financial journey has been shaped by her ability to reflect on her experiences. Despite facing numerous challenges early in her career, her reflection on those experiences helped her pivot into more strategic ventures, from media to philanthropy. Her financial wisdom, born out of reflection, has allowed her to not only amass wealth but also create lasting impact through her various endeavours.

Reflection brings closure and clarity, marking the end of one chapter while simultaneously laying the groundwork for what comes next. The sunset of a financial journey is not about regret or missed opportunities but about celebrating growth and applying those lessons for continued success. Through careful reflection, you gain the insight and wisdom needed to make more informed decisions, ensuring that your financial future remains bright even as one chapter closes.

As the sun sets on your current financial path, use this time to reflect, gain perspective, and build on the wisdom earned along the way—preparing yourself for the dawn of new opportunities and challenges that lie ahead.

Final Conclusion: The Financial Jungle – A Journey of Growth, Adaptation, and Mastery

As we reach the end of this journey through the financial jungle, we reflect on the lessons learned from the wild—each chapter revealing a new perspective on how to navigate the complexities of finance. Just as the animals of the savannah must rely on their unique strengths and survival instincts to thrive, so too must we draw from these principles to succeed in our own financial endeavors.

From the first rays of the **Sunrise**, where we laid the foundation by setting clear goals and building our financial base, to the challenges of droughts and predators, we have seen how adaptability, resilience, and strategic planning are essential for long-term success. Each creature we encountered—whether it was the antelope and wildebeests teaching us the value of collective movement or the buffalo demonstrating unwavering determination in the face of adversity—has offered critical insights for mastering the financial landscape.

The wild has shown us that financial success is not a sprint but a marathon. Like the patient **Elephant**, we learned the art of long-term planning and the importance of building a solid financial foundation that can weather storms and stand the test of time. We've also witnessed the stealth of the **Leopard**, teaching us the power of precision and calculated moves in finance, ensuring that each decision is targeted and strategic. And finally, we explored the world of the **Lion**, where we transitioned from surviving to thriving, from being a captive in our financial struggles to becoming a captor—taking control of our financial destiny with boldness and confidence.

But perhaps the most profound lesson comes at **Sunset**, where we are reminded to reflect on our journey, gaining wisdom from our experiences, and appreciating the milestones we've achieved along the way. Reflection brings the clarity needed to continue evolving, adjusting, and growing in an ever-changing financial world. It is through this wisdom that we build legacies—not just for ourselves but for future generations.

The financial jungle is vast and unpredictable, but by learning from nature, we develop the instincts and skills necessary to survive and thrive. Whether you are just beginning your journey or deep into the wilderness, remember that success requires patience, adaptability, resilience, and a relentless pursuit of your goals. Like the animals we've encountered, the financial world is a constant battle, but with the right strategies and mindset, you can emerge as a leader in your own financial kingdom.

As we close this chapter, take with you the lessons of the wild, and know that the jungle will always offer new opportunities to grow, evolve, and create lasting wealth. The path ahead may not always be clear, but with the knowledge gained from this journey, you are well-equipped to master the financial jungle and thrive in whatever comes your way.

About the Author

Kevin] is a financial analyst, strategist, and storyteller with a deep passion for both wealth-building and the raw, untamed beauty of nature. Fascinated by the intricate balance of ecosystems and the instincts that drive survival, Kevin found a striking parallel between the financial world and the laws of the wild. Just as every creature in the jungle must adapt, strategize, and endure, so too must individuals navigate the unpredictable terrain of wealth.

Blending financial expertise with a love for the natural world, Kevin crafted *The Jungle* as more than just a book—it's an invitation to see money through the lens of survival, resilience, and calculated action. Every chapter draws from the wisdom of the animal kingdom, offering readers practical financial lessons wrapped in the thrill of nature's greatest stories.

When not analyzing markets or exploring investment strategies, Kevin finds inspiration in the great outdoors—observing wildlife, trekking through landscapes, and marveling at the untold lessons hidden in the world around us.

Welcome to *The Jungle*—where the rhythm of nature meets the art of financial mastery.

www.ingramcontent.com/pod-product-compliance
Lightning Source LLC
LaVergne TN
LVHW022045200926
848481LV00003B/800
9798230201625